Raising
Finance

Grant Thornton advises Contender on the acquisition of Medusa, which combines two of the largest independent home entertainment distribution companies...

Grant Thornton

"Grant Thornton guided us with an expert hand throughout the entire transaction process. From innovative initial ideas on potential sources of funding, to a marathon completion meeting – they showed admirable commitment and energy."

**Charles Ogilvie
Finance Director
Contender Limited**

The combined group, which brings together two of the UK's largest independent home entertainment distribution companies will operate under the Contender Entertainment Group (CEG) banner.

Commenting on the deal, Thomas Dey, Senior Manager at Grant Thornton Corporate Finance said: "This deal represents an excellent strategic acquisition for CEG, and Grant Thornton are particularly pleased to have funded this acquisition entirely by debt."

To discuss your corporate finance requirements in confidence please call **David Ascott** or **Thomas Dey**.
Grant Thornton House
Melton Street
Euston Square
London NW1 2EP
T 020 7383 5100
W www.grant-thornton.co.uk

Flotations

Disposals

Raising Finance

Due Diligence

MBO/MBI

Mergers & Acquisitions

THE SUNDAY TIMES

BUSINESS ENTERPRISE GUIDE

Raising Finance

A Practical Guide to Starting, Expanding & Selling your Business

PAUL BARROW

RECOMMENDED BY

INSTITUTE OF DIRECTORS

KOGAN PAGE

London and Sterling, VA

This book has been endorsed by the Institute of Directors.

The endorsement is given to selected Kogan Page books which the IoD recognises as being of specific interest to its members and providing them with up-to-date, informative and practical resources for creating business success. Kogan Page books endorsed by the IoD represent the most authoritative guidance available on a wide range of subjects including management, finance, marketing, training and HR.

The views expressed in this book are those of the author and are not necessarily the same as those of the Institute of Directors.

Publisher's note
Every possible effort has been made to ensure that the information contained in this book is accurate at the time of going to press, and the publishers and authors cannot accept responsibility for any errors or omissions, however caused. No responsibility for loss or damage occasioned to any person acting, or refraining from action, as a result of the material in this publication can be accepted by the editor, the publisher or the author.

First published in Great Britain in 2004

Kogan Page Limited
120 Pentonville Road
London N1 9JN
United Kingdom
www.kogan-page.co.uk

The views expressed in this book are those of the author, and are not necessarily the same as those of Times Newspapers Ltd.

British Library Cataloguing in Publication Data

A CIP record for this book is available from the British Library.

ISBN 0 7494 4260 3

Typeset by JS Typesetting Ltd, Wellingborough, Northants
Printed and bound in Great Britain by Bell & Bain, Glasgow

Contents

Why use Total Finance Solutions

TFS is an independent Business Finance Consultancy whose aim is to assist individuals and SMEs to obtain the financial facilities required to expand and develop their business.

We provide creative capital solutions with unmatched personal service, and can fund any size of business loan or equipment lease quickly. We can find funding for loans that the banks won't approve, e.g. income/credit problems, start-ups, and property sale and leaseback.

Ways we can help
- Creative capital solutions with unmatched personal service
- Complete confidentiality guaranteed
- Free initial consultation
- Professionally packaged applications
- Any amount considered
- Can fund any type of loan or lease quickly, that the banks won't approve

Services

Commercial Mortgages
Mortgages for all types of business premises, including offices, industrial units, nursing homes, hotels, restaurants, public houses etc.

Equipment Leasing
Just about every type of equipment or vehicle can now be leased, new or old. There are also various tax and cash flow advantages. Ask about operating leases, contract hire, finance leases and lease purchase.

Land Development
Whether you are undertaking a new build development, or refurbishment of an existing property, we can finance the purchase of land and buildings, together with the development costs.

Asset Based Finance
Raise finance against machinery, plant, equipment and stock, releasing company worth into cash without further securities.

Equity Finance
Do you require funding for a new venture? Talk to us, we know the people to help you.

Property Sale & Leaseback
Release the equity in your commercial property by selling at an agreed price and leasing back with an option to buy back in the future. his product is of special benefit to MBO's and MBI's who have the opportunity to acquire business premises but don't have the necessary funding. Also suitable for owner-occupiers with a short to medium demand for working capital, but where a remortgage would not provide the required working capital.

Factoring & Invoice Discounting
Factoring provides cash flow via your sales invoices, without waiting 30-120 days for your hard earned money.

UNLOCK THE MYSTERY OF BORROWING

How to use this book

Please read the chapters in this book in any order you wish. It is not a novel, which relies on introducing the characters, building up the story and finally (hopefully) bringing it all to some exciting conclusion. Each chapter is complete in itself and does not rely on your having read an earlier chapter to make sense of it. I did think long and hard about the order of this book and maybe should have had the courage of my original convictions. However, I have opted for the more chronologically correct sequence of events: *growing, grooming, selling*. A large part of the book is devoted to grooming your business for sale and selling it. I make no apology for this because this is the logical end goal for most people who own a business. However, I have not entirely ignored using finance to fund value-adding growth activities.

My belief is that the best way to understand anything is to read a bit that explains how something is done, then see how another business did the same thing, and then finally reflect on your own business to see if this course of action is appropriate and how you will do it. A chapter may, for example, take as its theme equity funding. The first part of the chapter will discuss the issues, the options, the pros and cons, etc. This may then be illustrated with a real life example – what they did, where it worked for them and maybe where it did not. Finally the chapter will be rounded off with a summary and advice for your business to follow.

At the back of this book you will find a Glossary, which defines and explains the more technical words or expressions used in the book – just in case you have forgotten them. There is also a Sources of help section in which I have provided contact details for a whole raft of people and organisations that may be of use to you. You may feel confident to do most things yourself in the normal course of business but in some aspects of grooming and selling a business it does improve the process and increase your chances of success if you use the right specialists.

A few words of encouragement. I make my living helping owner-managers maximise the value in their businesses. One business that I had the pleasure of helping (it is mentioned in this book) had just over a year ago pulled out of negotiations to sell at the due diligence stage. It was a painful process and the asking price of £3 million was unachievable. Less than one year later with quite a small amount of help from me they had groomed the business for sale, prepared a killer information memorandum and sold the business for £8 million cash – all paid on completion. The sale process took less than two months and due diligence was completed painlessly in 10 days. Let this example be an encouragement to you. If this book helps you to achieve what you want from you business then we both will be very happy people. Good luck.

Acknowledgements

I don't want this to sound like a gushy Oscar acceptance speech but I do want to thank three distinct groups of people who have helped me substantially in the preparation and writing of this book.

First I would like to thank all the presenters and delegates on both the numerous Warwick Business School and Cranfield University programmes that I have been involved with over the last 15 years. Over this period I have seen some 500 business people pass through such programmes as the Business Growth Programme, Management Development Programme, and more recently the Value Forum. They have all been an inspiration to me both in the expertise that they have shared and the insight that they have given into their respective businesses. They have all had stories to tell, some of which I have been able to use in this book.

Next I would like to thank the handful of businesses that have allowed me to use them as case studies throughout this book – just over 20 in total. Some of these have provided me with some most intimate details of their business life. In many cases I have used their real names but in some cases I have felt it better to provide a degree of anonymity. However, all their experiences are relevant and help to illustrate many of the points and lessons to be learnt from the process of using other people's money to grow and ultimately sell businesses.

Finally I would like to thank those closer to home who have had to put up with me writing what must have appeared like a never-ending series of books over the last 18 months or so – in fact it has been only three books. Rachel, thank you for putting up with a husband who is forever bashing away on the laptop – trying to make sure I get my daily quota of 2,000 words written. You have always been encouraging and supportive. To Mark, my son, I extend a massive thanks for telling all your mates, so proudly, about his dad the writer and getting them to beg, borrow or steal (or even buy) my books. Keep up the good work – I'm proud of you. For both of you I have some bad news though – I feel another book (or two) coming on.

Introduction

If you have suffered the misfortune of reading books on growth, finance and business planning (and for my sins I have written books on most of these) you may have wondered where the book is that shows you how to put together a strategy to grow the value of your business, and ultimately sell it. Not just a textbook that talks about the theory – there are plenty of those – but a book that tells you how it really is and how it has (or has not) been done by some real businesses. This book is almost a work of faction – it mixes fact with fiction. The facts are the in-depth knowledge of how to raise money (every conceivable method – legal and otherwise) at the right time for your business to grow its value (not just its size); how to groom your business for sale and sell it for the best price possible; the experiences of some real life businesses that have been down this route. The fiction is that the names (both company and individuals) have been changed – mostly to respect their privacy otherwise they would never have spilled the beans to me.

There are three main threads to this book: growing, grooming and selling. The first is concerned with developing a financial strategy for your growing business *(growing)*.

There is an old expression that says that any port in a storm will do. Many UK businesses find that the storm drives them towards the same old port for money – the bank overdraft. But what do our European competitors do? Surveys have shown that they use a far wider range of finance. The survey data in Figure 0.1 were compiled by 3i/Cranfield European Enterprise Centre and compare how UK and French small and medium-sized enterprises (SMEs) were funded. They make very interesting reading.

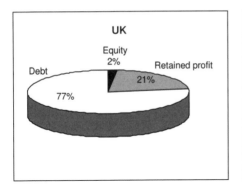
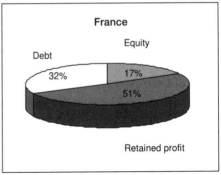

Figure 0.1 How SMEs are funded in the UK and France

The figures show quite clearly that while UK SMEs used predominantly bank borrowing (77 per cent) our French competitors were far less reliant on the banks (32 per cent). In difficult times, such as recessions, this gives the French a quite clear advantage – far fewer loan repayments to make when profits are low.

How then did our larger businesses compare to their French counterparts? I think you will notice quite a change. It seems to show that as our UK SMEs grow they tend to develop a more sophisticated funding spread, relying far less on borrowed money. This seems (to me) to be a better funding strategy to cope with recessions.

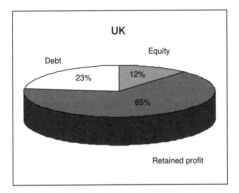
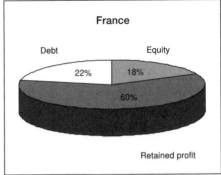

Figure 0.2 How larger businesses are funded in the UK and France

Figure 0.2 shows UK and French larger businesses are on a level footing, with more reliance on equity and reserves to fund their businesses – the UK 77 per cent and France 78 per cent.

Ok, so the Europeans appear to be a bit more savvy when it comes to planning the finances of their businesses, but how well do they do as a result? Well, over the last decade the number of businesses grew in mainland Europe while there has been a large decline in the UK. Also, look at the widespread invasion of European (and American) businesses into the UK to steal both market share and ownership of nearly all of our utility companies. This makes me think that they are doing something right. Maybe we can learn from both them and some of the more successful UK businesses.

The second thread is developing a strategy that adds maximum value to your business *(grooming)*.

Many UK businesses have no strategy at all, probably because their owners do not know what they want. As a consequence they just drift along on the back of their customers and the passive support of their bankers. These businesses will for the most part fail or just cease trading – losing most of the value that the business has delivered to date. In contrast, a small number of businesses are entirely focused and do only those things that add value to the business. As a consequence these businesses do not blindly chase growth in the vain hope that it will maximise their value. They will, under the right circumstances, turn away some profitable business opportunities that other businesses would give their back teeth for. Why do they do this? Because the cost of the additional investment will far outweigh the value added to the business within the timescale set by the owners of the business.

Of course some of you may be thinking that profit growth is the only way to add maximum value to a business. You are only partly correct. The fact is that it is not always clear as to what business activity will maximise the value in a business unless you have a clear picture (vision?) of what you want to achieve. The key, therefore, to maximising value in a business is to know what end result you want and within which timescale. If a business sale is at the end of this process we call this 'grooming for sale'. If, however, no sale is on the horizon we call this 'building value'. Only then can you embark on the correct strategy to deliver these.

The third strand is realising the value in your business *(selling)*. All businesses have a finite life – especially owner-managed businesses. I would struggle to think of more than a handful of businesses that have lasted more than 200 years. Many of these have had several different owners during this time. Consequently it is right and proper to think of bringing your ownership of your business to an end – how else will you realise the value in your business? Do not confuse this with bringing the business to an end – employees, suppliers and customers will survive. In fact in many cases the business will thrive and go on to deliver improved value for its new owners.

However, selling a business needs to be managed to maximise the value you will receive. What is the correct price for your business? I have known businesses to sell for twice the original estimate of their value. Who should you sell to, to achieve the best deal – management, trade sale, venture capitalist? Who do you need in your corner to help you – accountant, lawyer, sales agent? How do you let buyers know your business is for sale – networking or an advert in the *Financial Times*?

1   *Value – what is it all about?*

Some basic rules on creating value

I suppose before you embark on reading a book that has as its objective creating, maximising and realising value we ought to set down some ground rules. This book does not cover the following: business planning, strategy and finance. There are, fortunately, enough good books on these aspects of business (that's my quick plug for the other business guides in this series out of the way early on). This book has a very narrow focus. It examines how business people create, maximise and realise value within their business. However, to achieve all of these you will need to understand and have a plan, a valid strategy and some understanding of finance.

Let's get back to basics. Why did you go into business in the first place? Perhaps you lost your job or thought you could do better than your old employers. Maybe you had invented something and wanted to commercialise it yourself. Whatever reason it was, you either drifted into self-employment or were pushed. Look at yourself now and the business you have. How much has it changed? How many people do you employ? Are your products and services innovative and fresh? Do you make good profits? Are you getting grief from the bank?

In an unsubtle way I guess I am asking the question: do you have a business that someone could say has some value – sufficient for them to pay good money for? I would hazard a guess that if your business has changed little over the years and still employs just you, it has no value. You make think I am being a little harsh, especially if it has made you a reasonable living over the time you have been involved in it and you have a few quid in the bank as a result. You may have friends who envy your lifestyle and the fact that you are your own boss but in reality you could not sell your business – it has no value.

Please do not be offended – I am in exactly the same boat. In fact, it frightens me because as is the case with lots of other business people, my business only has value to me and only while I am physically and mentally fit to run it. However, I think we are establishing the first two rules of value:

1. someone other than you as the business owner must be prepared to recognise that value and be prepared to hand over good money for it; and

2. if that value is still dependent on your being involved in the business this will reduce any value the business may have. In most cases it will negate most or all of the business value.

Beauty is in the eye of the beholder (in this case the buyer)

Ok, let's move the debate on a little. What is it that creates this value in a business – sufficient for someone else to say, 'Hey, I like your business and I want to buy it.' To answer this I want you to have an 'out of body' experience – yes, I want you to imagine you are buying your own business. What value would you place on it and how have you arrived at that figure? Let me try and imagine what your thought process might be. First, you are listening to the owner telling you about the business:

- Umm – where do I start?

- Well, I know it made £20,000 profit last year so it's got to be worth at least that.

- The business owns some computers and a car, which have a book value of £10,000 so these must be worth something.

- The business has £20,000 in the bank so someone will give me pound for pound for this.

- I have got over 250 customers who buy off me on a regular basis – surely this must be worth something, but I don't know what. This year this has given me an annual sales figure of £500,000.

- I own my own factory/office, which is big enough for now, although I am not sure whether it would be big enough if turnover were to increase substantially. It cost me £200,000 but has a mortgage of £180,000, which will take me another 19 years to pay off.

- I have got three good people working for me who I have had for years, but without me being there I am not sure how long they could keep the business going.

- Our new product, the 611GT, has all the bells and whistles and beats the socks of the competition.

- Umm – what else can I say, and what value do I place value on that? At least £250,000 I would think. Surely that's fair for 10 years' hard work?

As the buyer, how do you assimilate this and place a value on this business? I do not at this stage intend to go through how to value a business – we will look at this later. However, as the buyer your thought process may be as follows:

- Umm – looks a bit small for me this business, but let's wait and see what the owner has to say about it.

- £20,000 profit last year: looks a bit marginal to me. If it had a bad debt one year it would wipe out all the profit.

- Computers and a car, which have a book value of £10,000. If I bought this business I don't need any more cars and computer equipment so I would have to sell them – probably make a loss on them.

- £20,000 in the bank. That'll do nicely but I aim to get that at a discount to partly compensate for some of the other rubbish that comes with the business.

- 250 regular customers producing an annual sales figure of £500,000. Oh my goodness, all those customers to service just to make a small profit. Just as I thought: turnover is a bit small for me.

- Factory/office with £20,000 apparent equity. If I were to buy this business I would want to relocate it to my site. This leaves me with a building that may be a pain to sell, especially as it is probably too small for most commercial use and change of use may not be possible to get.

- Three people working who have been there for years and no management. If I did buy the business how much would it cost me in redundancy payments to get rid of them? Bit of problem this, being an owner-managed business – how pally is he with the customers and will they walk if he is no longer part of the business? May have to employ him for 12 months as a bit of insurance – although I don't really want him as he will not fit in with my organisation.

- New product, the 611GT, has all the bells and whistles and beats the socks of the competition. Now I do like that and to be honest it would be the only sound reason for buying the business. My concern is who owns the intellectual rights, patents, trademarks, etc – the business or the individual? Need to sort this one out.

- Umm – a bit difficult this but on balance, despite the 611GT, I think this could be more trouble than it's worth. Walks off saying, 'Sorry, but I don't think I can make you an offer that reflects the value you may think the business has and I don't want to insult you with what you may think is a derisory offer.'

Do you see the picture? Obviously the owner is just too close to the business and cannot take a dispassionate view of its value. He places value on those things that he has toiled over the years to build up. Let's not be critical – we would all be just as guilty under similar circumstances. That's why it makes sense to get an outsider to assess the value of a business – it is helpful to get a truly independent expert opinion. They will assess the value in a clinical way and according to a tried and tested process. As a result you will get consistency since they will use predetermined measures to value the business – profitability, customer base, balance sheet strength, etc.

This is a great starting point as it will give you a guide price as to what an average buyer might pay for your business today in its current state. You can then decide whether this matches up with your expectations or not and make an appropriate decision. However, at the end of the day, independent experts (valuers) do not usually buy businesses. They can be a bit like estate agents – they believe they know the current market place for businesses like yours and can place a value on it that, a) matches up with what you want to hear (ie high) to get your business, or b) is on the low side to ensure a quick sale to get their commission. So be careful.

I know it is blindingly obvious but buyers buy businesses and they are all, by and large, different. If they are serial buyers then they have established a model that is successful for them – usually based on previous failures. My experience is that when you buy your first business you generally get it wrong – pay too much and it is the wrong business for you. The second business that you buy does not go so badly wrong – maybe bought at a better price, but you fail to capitalise on the opportunity. It is not until about your fourth business acquisition that you get it right. This means most buyers have a clear idea of what constitutes value to them and it is different for all of them according to their circumstances and experiences. It is also argued that a trade buyer will usually pay a higher price than an investment buyer. This is usually attributed to the fact that a trade buyer is familiar with the industry and can see the potential within a business and will make the changes needed to improve its value. It is said that an investment buyer is merely a collector who buys as seen and makes no significant change to its value, hence the need to buy at a 'good price'.

This leads us to understanding the third and fourth rules of value:

3. unless you are brutally honest you cannot truly place a true value on your own business; and

4. the value of your business is ultimately dependent on the characteristics of your buyer.

When to sell?

At this stage you may well be saying to yourself that maximising the value of your business is an impossible task because you are likely to focus on the wrong things and that you can have no influence over your buyer's attitudes. Do not be so pessimistic: I have given you some very valuable clues. First, do not forget all the usual good business practice – customer focus, efficiency, healthy pricing, investment analysis, people management, etc. These must be universal truths under all circumstances. However, when it comes down to the very narrow business of maximising the value of your business, we are looking at a further refinement. You need to understand where your business is in its value lifecycle. It's quite simple, because a business will go through the following stages:

- start-up business – little value but plenty of potential;
- early/late growth business – low to moderate value with potential more clearly identified;
- established business – potentially maximum value with reduced potential for growth;
- failing business – low value with some potential;
- terminal business – little value with questionable potential.

Start-up business

Sorry to disappoint you, but by and large there is not much of a market for second-hand start-up businesses – especially those that failed in the dotcom stock market fiasco. There *is* a market for some businesses that succeed start-up but which have not got past the first rung of early growth. However, valuing them is very subjective since there is no real market or financial performance data on which to make a reasoned judgement. In this case the value is entirely based on what the buyer believes they can do with the business. As a value-maximising strategy I cannot recommend planning to sell at start-up.

Early/late growth business

If your objective is to sell your business within the next one to three years, then you should aim to get it to somewhere between an early growth and an established business. You could almost call this late growth. Table 1.1 shows the historic financial performance for a business for 2001 to 2003 together with some estimates for 2004 and 2005.

Table 1.1   Financial performance for a 'late growth' business 2001–2003 and estimates for 2004–5

	2001	2002	2003	2004?	2005?
Sales	250,000	500,000	1,000,000	2,000,000	4,000,000
Gross Profit	100,000	210,000	430,000	900,000	1,840,000
Overheads	100,000	150,000	200,000	250,000	300,000
Net Profit	**0**	**60,000**	**230,000**	**650,000**	**1,540,000**

Of course you will notice that on the face of it you will not have maximised the value at this stage. On the basis of 2003 profits and using a profit multiple of, say 10, then a valuation of the business could be £2,300,000 (10 x £230,000). Not bad you may say. However, assuming continued sales growth at the same rate together with some slight improvements in gross and overhead escalation, the same business could be valued at £15,400,000 (10 x £1,540,000) based on 2005 estimates. Wow, you may think – but remember the business has yet to achieve the 2004 and 2005 levels of performance anticipated. As the seller you may happily sell the business for £5 million – that is at least twice what it was worth at the end of 2003. Since there is unlikely to be any significant net asset position due to low profitability this looks a pretty good deal.

Fortunately this is not usually a problem, as most buyers prefer to buy businesses at this stage. Why? Because it gives them an excellent way in which to justify it to their board, bank, external investors, etc. They can say that they are buying a great business at a good price from which they can extract even more value. In effect they will say they have bought a £15 million business for £5 million – not bad. They will claim that they can do this through good management, synergy, etc. The truth is that like a good stock market investment, they have bought at the lower end with plenty of growth potential left. As long as they do not completely balls it up, they should benefit from the growth and value improvement that mildly competent management should bring.

We will look at an early/late growth business later in the book, which was sold purely on expectation and greed based on one good year of trading profit.

Established business

Of course those of you who are sitting on established businesses will be closing the pages of this book now, thinking you have missed the boat – don't, because you haven't missed it. The challenge is that you have is to demonstrate that it has consistently deliverable value. In other words, you trade off potential improved value for demonstrable repeatable value. Table 1.2 shows the historic financial performance for a business for the years 2000 to 2003 together with some estimates for 2004.

Table 1.2 Financial performance for an 'established' business 2001–2003 and estimates for 2004

	2000	**2001**	**2002**	**2003**	**2004?**
Sales	2,000,000	2,100,000	2,205,000	2,315,250	2,431,013
Gross Profit	800,000	861,000	926,100	995,558	1,069,646
Overheads	100,000	105,000	110,250	115,763	121,551
Net Profit	**700,000**	**756,000**	**815,850**	**879,795**	**948,095**

Unless one has some insider knowledge both of the business and the industry, one would conclude that this business has settled into middle age and essentially stopped growing – annual sales growth has leveled off at 5 per cent. There has been some modest improvement in gross profit and overheads have crept up by 5 per cent each year. This business would appear to have little apparent potential so a buyer would not be paying for this. This would be reflected in a lower profit multiple of, say, 7. On the basis of 2003 profits and using a profit multiple of 7 then a valuation of the business could be £6,158,565 (7 x £879,795). Not bad you may say. Looking just one year on, this business could quite easily be valued at £6,636,665 (7 x £948,095). You might well sell this business for £6.5 million based on profits alone.

However, there is another factor to be taken into account in a business at this stage of its value life – the balance sheet. A business that has made over

£3 million in profits over four years is a big business. It will have net assets of at least £3 million, more if we take into account the previous years of profit generation. These net assets will comprise, possibly, land and buildings, equipment, debtors, stock, cash in the bank, etc. These all have a value to a purchaser. Let's say that these are absolutely essential to the running of the business, in which case a buyer may well offer 90 per cent value on them. This adds another £2.7 million plus to the selling price. In total the business may well be worth just over £9 million.

The buyer has no problem justifying this purchase. There is very little risk – the business has a proven track record of strong profit and (probably) cash generation. About a third of the purchase price is acquiring assets, which the banks will like. The remaining two-thirds will be recovered out of about six years' profits – even if the new buyer does nothing much to improve it. However, chances are that as part of a bigger group some synergy exists – common salesforce, centralised accounting, group senior management, etc. This could reduce the payback period to four or five years. Very nice indeed!

Later in this book we will look at an established owner-managed business, which was very carefully marketed and snapped up by a competitor.

Failing business

Essentially this covers businesses that are not profitable but have been trading for some years. The net asset position could be quite significant, especially if the decline has happened only in the last couple of years. Again these businesses can have considerable value based on what a buyer can do by merging the target business into their own to improve overall profit generation and asset stripping. While a declining business is usually a sign of business failure, to the right buyer it can have a value in excess of a profitable business. Extracting this value is difficult and usually requires the help of a specialist intermediary to find a buyer.

A modern day example of this type of business could be Marconi, whose troubles have been widely publicised. One could argue that by diversifying and selling off what had now become 'non-core' (unexciting some might say) but nevertheless profitable activities, the board of directors have unwittingly destroyed the value of the business. Those of you with reasonably long memories of the old GEC under Lord Weinstock and his renowned cash mountain will understand the tragedy that has occurred to this once proud and long-established business.

We will look at a failing business later in the book, which was quite quickly devoured by a competitor at a good price – certainly far in excess of its apparent value.

Terminal business

This includes a wide range of potential business failures. Essentially these may be businesses that are sound but have too much debt or have reached the end of their natural life, for example the product/service is no longer viable, or a skilled workforce is no longer available. If failure is due to poor financing then value can be protected, or at least not totally lost, by replacing all or some of the debt with fresh equity.

We will not be covering terminal businesses in this book because by and large the value in them is quite negligible (from an outsider's perspective) and most funding options are not available to this type of business. However, if your business falls into this category then may I suggest that you read *The Bottom Line* (see Sources of help). You should specifically read the sections on profitability, cash flow and short-term funding. You may find some of the chapter on debt-bound and failing businesses helpful.

A few final thoughts on value

In the Introduction I stated that much of this book is about getting your business ready to sell. I would like to adopt one of Covey's Seven Habits: 'Begin with the end in mind', which is very appropriate. The end in mind for most business owners must be to ultimately sell their business. To this extent everything you do in your business must be targeted at achieving this objective. Timescales suddenly take on a new importance – if you want to sell up in, say, two years, make sure that all your business decisions have maximum payback within this time. This does not totally mean thinking short term – it means being realistic.

However, what you must remember is that most businesses need to go through some form of evolution to get to the stage at which they can maximise the value in the business. Small businesses seldom offer maximum value. This means that some degree of growth is probably implicit in most businesses' plans to maximise value. In many cases the use of external financing may help accelerate this process – something that is covered in this book.

Selling your business can make you feel like a nervous bridegroom (or bride for that matter) approaching the finality (as it seems to some) of the wedding day. Wedding day nerves can creep in and perhaps there is just the chance that either you or your intended spouse might not turn up on the day – a change of heart perhaps? It is the same with selling your business, especially one that you have created and lived with for many years. Do not underestimate the wrench and mental turmoil that surround selling your business. Questions like, 'Have I got the best price?' and, 'What will I do with my life now I have no business to run?' will spring to mind. I can help you with the first of these but sorry, you are on your own when it comes to life after business – although I can give you some basic guidance on making sure you have met your likely income and capital requirements.

A final thought for now. I heard someone pose a very good question to a client of mine who is looking at selling his business. My client asked, 'How do I know if I have got the best price for my business?' The other person thought for a moment or two and responded, 'When you would not buy back your own business for the amount you have just sold it for.' What an excellent answer, I thought.

2

Start-up financing

Small and medium-sized enterprise (SME) start-ups

Case study: advertising agency

I recall the first business that I was involved in setting up. There were three of us, and our objective was to build a small regional advertising agency servicing the needs of what we believed to be a 'captive' market. We already knew our customers – they were the clients of our associated business. We already had most of the people that we needed; what we did not have was very much money or any premises. To all intents and purposes we were a typical start-up except that we had another business – some might dispute whether that was a help or not. Without going into all the business details we had a rough ride for about three years. Our business could feature in almost all the chapters of this book – start-up, growth, financial collapse, recovery, and ultimately disposal.

So how did we get this business going? We did the boring thing – we produced a very brief business plan. Effectively it was a budget or profit forecast for the next 12 months and a 'guestimate' of what years two and three might look like if we grew the business as we anticipated. We listed all the known customers we had (or assumed we would get) and the amount of business we thought they would put our way in the first 12 months. I have to say it looked pretty good. Even with just this known business we were on course to make a healthy profit in year one.

The real problem was that our set-up costs were too much for us to finance ourselves. If I remember correctly, we needed about £20,000 for equipment and about £10,000 to acquire and set up a basic office. Later we realised we needed some money for working capital – about £15,000 by our estimates. We were bringing to the pot expertise, hopefully some clients, some key people, and about £10,000 in cash.

Acquiring premises

I don't want to bore you with the detail but there were costs that suddenly appeared as we got further down the road. We thought that getting a lease on a small office nearby would be quite straightforward. Since none of us was a solicitor we used a local solicitor to check out the lease being offered to us by the landlord. This was to cost us £1,000 – and to this day we are not sure whether it was worth it. The landlord wanted to tie us in for five years. In addition there was a rent review after three years with upward-only increments. This meant that there was a good chance that after three years our rent could go up by between 20 and 50 per cent based on current (at that time) rental rises. Then just for good measure the landlord wanted personal guarantees from the directors, because the limited company that we had set up was new. We did not fully understand it at the time but the landlord wanted us to undertake a personal guarantee that was 'jointly and severally' on all three directors.

Let me just take a brief moment to tell you about the horrors of the true nature of the words 'jointly and severally'. Some of you may think (as did we at the time) that this means that we would all equally share the responsibility to pay the landlord if the business could not pay the rent. Well that's just the start of it. The real twist, is what if one or more of my co-directors could not pay their share – because they had gone bust or had no spare cash? The answer is that the other director(s) remain fully liable for the full amount. In the worst-case scenario, if my co-directors could not pay up I would end up being responsible for paying the landlord in full. This can be a severe test of any friendship.

Oh, and by the way, the landlord imposed a few other restrictions on us that did not appear to be so important at the time. Initially we were not permitted to sub-let any part of the premises, but after some negotiation we were allowed to do so – but even then we were still responsible for the rental payments (just in case the sub-tenant did not pay up). We were not allowed to assign the lease, which meant that even if we had found another tenant who would pay the rent we as a company, and ultimately the three of us as guarantors, were still liable if the new tenant did not pay up. Finally, for good measure we had to pay a premium of £5,000 to get this wonderful property under these terms! A word of advice – be careful when you are taking up a lease: learn from our mistakes.

We hoped that our bank would help us with financing all the costs of acquiring our offices.

Capital equipment

This was the easy bit because we pretty much knew what we wanted. We had prepared our shopping list and all the equipment was going to cost us £50,000. This included a small telephone system, tables and chairs, computers, printers, software, etc. Even though we knew that these were one-off expenses we were horrified at the cost. This stopped us in our tracks and forced us into a re-think. Could we buy some of these things second-hand? In the end we bought our tables and chairs from a furniture auction and picked up a second-hand telephone system. The computer system was too critical to our business to buy used – we needed the latest specification equipment and that was unlikely to be available used. Also, we needed the security of a warranty just in case anything went wrong (and it did!)

We also questioned our needs. Did everyone need a computer? Could some people have lower spec computers? Could we cut down on phones? This got us looking at the value that this spend was going to bring to the business. Remember that there must be a value payback for every penny spent. What we did was look more closely at our plan to see when we expected to grow and take on more business – this would be the driver for taking on more people. We saw that from day one there would just be three of us but that this would rise to five in between six and nine months' time. We had been lulled into thinking we needed computers, tables, chairs, phones, etc for five people all in one go – hence our original budget of £50,000. But now we knew that we could put off a significant amount of this spend – two persons' worth – for six months. Why spend all the money now when there was no immediate payback, no value created? We also knew that in six to nine months' time when we took on another two people that things would change again – computer specs improve, possibly become cheaper, our needs change, etc. It made sense not to commit ourselves today for a future need that might change.

In the end we cut down our capital budget to £20,000 – a worthwhile saving. This was going to be split as shown in Table 2.1.

Table 2.1   Capital budget

Tables and chairs (used)	£1,000
Telephone system (used)	£750
Software (new)	£5,000
Computers, printers, network, etc	£13,250

We congratulated ourselves on cutting our capital spend from £50,000 to £20,000. The next problem was, who was going to help us fund this? Our immediate thoughts yet again fell to the bank – although we also thought that hire purchase or leasing might be possible.

Working capital

I was asked by John O'Donell to contribute to an article he was writing for the business section in *The Sunday Times* – it's always nice to get your name in the papers. He asked me, 'What are the usual mistakes that people make when preparing a business plan?' and as a second question, 'What advice would you have for anyone writing a business plan?' To the first question I responded something like this. I find that people are over-optimistic about two things – when sales will be achieved, and when they will be paid. These are big mistakes. I explained to him that usually people start by making some sort of estimate of what they may sell for the following year – nothing wrong with that because you have to start somewhere. However, what is wrong is the way they expect these sales to come in – in a linear method. The sales forecast in Table 2.2 gives a good example of this. All figures are in £000s.

Table 2.2 Usually wrong sales trend

Month	1	2	3	4	5	6	7	8	9	10	11	12	Total
Sales	10	10	10	10	10	10	10	10	10	10	10	10	120

Here you can see that an annual sales figure of £120,000 has been spread evenly over the next 12 months ahead – does this look right for a start-up business? My experience is that you cannot just turn on the tap and expect sales to march along to some rigid order like that shown in the table. I bet that in the first month of a new business, sales will be minimal – unless you have some already contracted. Certainly they will be well below break-even and it may take four to six months to achieve good levels of sales. In reality the picture should be more progressive, something like that shown in Table 2.3.

Table 2.3 Nearer the truth sales trend

Month	1	2	3	4	5	6	7	8	9	10	11	12	Total
Sales	2	4	6	8	10	10	11	12	13	14	15	15	120

Here you can see that there is a gradual build-up in sales, which is how it works in reality. It is not until the fifth month that better than break-even sales can be achieved. Sales growth then goes through a slower phase until it plateaus in months 11 and 12. Some businesses may operate in a market that has strong seasonality, eg Christmas hampers, firework sales, overseas holidays, Easter eggs. In each of these cases the sales forecast will have its own progressive and peaking sales trend.

Perhaps now you can see why I believe that those people who prepare their sales forecast, and hence their subsequent profit forecast, on a linear basis, will almost inevitably get it wrong and be too optimistic about when their sales come in.

My second observation was to do with cash flow – the fact that cash always comes in slower than you think. Let me give you an example. In many business situations 30 days from date of invoice is the common terms on which credit is given. (By the way, do make sure to tell your customers what your terms of business and credit terms are – otherwise they will dream up their own, like paying you when they get round to it.) So on, say, 15 June, you sell something to your customer. If you are really quick on your invoicing then you send your invoice out within seven days – well done you, give yourself a pat on the back. If, however, you are like 75 per cent of businesses, your invoice goes out at the end of the month.

What do you do next? You get on with your normal business life and forget about this invoice. Some time later, probably a month after you sent out the invoice, you think that you could really use that cash. Only then do you start the process of debtor (cash) collection. You find out (after several phone calls) that the invoice went astray and you are asked to send a copy invoice – you are back to square one in the payment cycle. Perhaps you get my drift. Cash always takes longer to come in than you originally planned – unless you are absolutely red hot on sending out your invoices early (with the job, ideally) and begin chasing the debt before it becomes overdue.

Just as a point of interest, there have been numerous surveys on how long UK companies take to get paid – especially SMEs. It is getting better, thanks to an improving economic climate, low interest rates and government pressure. However, on average it still takes your typical SME in the UK around 60 days to get paid – almost twice their normal credit terms.

Perhaps you can now see why I told John O'Donell of *The Sunday Times* that I thought most people preparing business plans were too optimistic about when their cash would be coming in. In fact I suggested that people should prepare an A and B plan and assume that plan B would happen. Plan A is based on the hoped for situation – sales come in as planned and cash follows accordingly. Plan B is based on no business coming for three months and the cash for that taking a further two months to come in. This is not quite the worst-case scenario but it is really unpleasant – no cash for five months.

Case study: advertising agency (contd)

So, coming back to our business and the plan we were putting together, we did some of this. Unfortunately sales were even slower in coming in – but that's another story. We added to our sales forecast our running costs to show a profit forecast. We also prepared a cash flow forecast that showed when we would get paid, when we would have to pay suppliers, staff and the VAT man, and the effect this would have on our bank balance (or overdraft, as it was looking). Our figures showed that despite thinking our business was 'self-funding' we reckoned we needed about £15,000 to tide us over – to pay the rent, wages, etc before the money came rolling in. Let me tell you something – there is no similarity between the profit forecast and the cash flow forecast. If they look similar, ie profit = cash, then you have almost certainly made a mistake. In all probability your profit forecast will be about right but your cash flow forecast (if it shows bags of money in the bank towards the end of the year) is almost certainly wrong. I could spend a whole chapter on forecasting – but I won't: read my book *The Bottom Line*.

Once again we looked to the bank for financial support – probably a bank overdraft. You don't have to be too bright to see that we were relying an awful lot on the bank – either for an overdraft or loans. In total we needed £45,000 to start up our business – we could put in £10,000 so we needed to borrow about £35,000. We'll look at the options we considered in a bit more detail, and some of the ones we did not. But first we should just briefly look at another type of start-up that is comparatively rare but does occur.

Large-scale start-ups

So far we have looked at what might be termed a modest start-up – most businesses are like this. However, some business start-ups do not fit into this mould – they are large. This is usually because the start-up costs reflect the size of the potential market (national or even international); the service (high costs to set up and provide); or the uncertainty of income (hence the need to provide working capital, for several years in some cases). Recent examples of these have been the well-known Internet companies – there do not seem to be any notable manufacturing start-ups to speak of.

These are by their nature high-risk propositions. Of course the same process of business planning must be gone through as for a SME – it's just that the numbers (funding, people, resources) are bigger. In these start-up situations almost all the money is raised as equity funding – or risk capital as it is known. This comes either in the form of venture capital or IPO (Initial Public Offering). In the former case shares are not offered to the public but are bought by an investment organisation (the venture capital company). In the latter case the shares are made available to the public via either a prospectus (for a listing on the full Stock Exchange) or a placing document (for a listing on AIM, which is the second-tier Stock Exchange). These types of funding strategy are covered in Chapter 4 in this book.

The funding options

Let's look at the funding options available. Remember, you should be looking to have a funding strategy, even as a start-up business. The principle is that you should match the funding type (loans, overdraft, HP, etc) to the appropriate funding need (capital, other one-off start-up costs, working capital, etc). My experience is that when you are starting up a business any port in a storm will do, and that storm usually leads to the port called 'bank overdraft'. It makes sense to look at this first. Just as an aside I should point out that these funding options are not exclusively for start-up businesses – they can and are used by businesses at all stages in their lives.

Bank overdraft

Despite what most business people think, an overdraft is not forever – or so the banks believe. An overdraft is:

- A form of loan that has no formal capital repayments – the business only has to make interest payments for the period that it has the loan. Interest is payable on a daily basis at a rate that fluctuates according to the bank's base rate plus a mark-up (profit for the bank). This gives uncertainty over the cost – it will go up if interest rates go up. The interest paid is an allowable expense against business profits.

- Short term – to cover a temporary shortage of cash, eg start-up/ ongoing working capital.

- Quick and relatively cheap to set up. As a guide, if you just want a couple of thousand pounds then a phone call will usually suffice. If, however, you wanted £20,000 then a written application and business plan (usually using the bank's pack) will be needed. Please remember that each manager (or grade of manager, more importantly) has ceilings on how much they can lend.

- Annually renewed by the bank. Your overdraft facility will be reviewed by the bank and a renewal fee charged.

- Repayable on demand. In theory and in practice (when banks get nervous) all overdraft facilities can be withdrawn. There has been a move recently for some banks to 'guarantee' overdrafts, ie if you do not abuse the facility the bank cannot withdraw it.

- May involve fees. Usually a bank will charge you a flat fee for setting up an overdraft according to a sliding scale – this would certainly be applicable for larger overdraft facilities. However, many banks will offer free overdrafts when you move to them, say for two years, up to a certain limit.

- Usually secured on business or personal assets. Banks are in the business of secured lending – they are not risk-takers. Consequently, if you wanted to borrow, say, £50,000 then they will want to know that if you cannot repay the loan they can sell off your assets for at least enough to pay off the loan.

- It can be very difficult to increase an overdraft limit once it has been agreed with the bank – not very flexible when businesses are trying to grow.

Ok, so that's the bare bones of your typical bank overdraft facility, but what are some people's experiences of using an overdraft? I remember someone saying that if you owe the bank £20,000 they have got you by the b***s, but if you owe them £10 million you have got them by the b***s. There is some sort of truth in this statement so I will give you two examples that I know of.

Case study: car restoration business

Baroque was a small specialist car restoration business (American cars predominantly) based in a small industrial unit in Stratford upon Avon. Run by a husband and wife team and three mechanics/bodywork restorers they struggled for all the time that I knew them to make a profit and manage their overdraft. Throughout the two years that I worked with the business, the bank (no names, no pack drill) was constantly on their back – wanting figures (cash flow and profit projections); asking them daily what value of cheques were going to be paid in; asking them to come into the branch to interrogate them about the business (during business hours), etc.

They had what I would call a pitifully small overdraft, of just £7,500 – they had no other source of external funding and little remaining owners' equity. It was secured only on debtors because that was the only business asset – there were no personal assets. Most of the time the business really needed an overdraft closer to £12,000 and was constantly over its agreed limit. A regular feature of life was that the bank bounced cheques, charging a fee for this and constantly (so it seemed to us) to question how the owners were running the business. At the same time the bank was trying to force them to buy their products – pensions, critical illness cover, etc – which seemed an irrelevancy when the business was in trouble.

Not a happy ship. The tragedy was that just as the business was beginning to make a profit and grow, the bank pulled the plug – they got nothing back. We blamed the bank manager because he did not have the power to make the decisions we wanted – he always said that he would have to run things past his boss for a decision. We sensed they were not prepared to go the extra yard with the business.

How do you think the bank saw the situation? The manager was a small (or local) business manager so he had limited support (no assistant), had a lending ceiling of £7,500, and had failed to meet the bank's security requirements. He was feeling uncomfortable and things were getting worse – the business wanted more money. This would mean filling in forms and sending the matter 'upstairs', and since he could not put forward a good business case he was not going to do it – why put your head on the block for a hopeless case? He was working on containment and hoping against hope that somehow the situation would get better. If things got worse he would have to pull the plug, which was the only sensible banking option.

All in all a sorry tale, but what can you draw from this? I think the key points are:

- The lowest tier of bank manager is a powerless messenger – he or she processes information and passes it to centralised risk assessment departments. The manager then has to tell the customer the good or the bad news.

- Most bank managers are salespeople – they all have performance contracts to meet based on selling bank product/services. If they do not meet their contract targets they do not get pay rises or bonuses, and in tough times they are the first to lose their jobs.

- Most bank managers do not have any real understanding of what is going on in their customers' businesses – all they see is the daily cash movements. Based on this limited information they try to make lending decisions.

- The bank manager in the case study does not feel comfortable with the business and does not trust the judgement of the owners. The lending was 'hard core' with no movement, ie at the beginning, middle and end of the month the account was always in overdraft and at, near or above the agreed limit.

- Banks are extremely risk-aversive and subject to changing policies as the economy changes – any sniff of a recession or poor trading and they want their money back. In this business they felt very vulnerable since it had no other form of funding – the bank is on its own in their eyes.

- At this level you always feel very conscious of the fact that the bank wants asset cover for all lending – eg if they have lent you £7,500 they want to be sure that you have business or personal assets worth at least £15,000 to cover this.

Case study: marketing business

As a contrast I know a marketing business employing just over 30 people, which enjoys an entirely different relationship with its bank. Their size dictates that they have a corporate manager, who has an assistant who performs analysis on their customers' businesses. They have far greater scope to make lending decisions and they understand their customers better. Even though turnover of the marketing company is under £2 million (they have no significant media business) they have an overdraft facility in excess of £100,000 and use a wide range of other financing facilities. This business had won regional awards for its creativity and had been rated highly in a recent financial survey of regional advertising agencies by a leading firm of accountants. It had always been profitable and was going through a period of exciting growth, while other agencies, both regional and national, were suffering.

On a day-to-day basis they do not really notice their bank exists. There is no evidence of interference. The directors are keen to involve the bank and each year send the manager (who they like and trust) a fresh business plan. Every year (at least) their manager comes out to see how they are doing and the annual overdraft review appears to be a formality. They feel that their manager is supportive and prepared to run some risk, if necessary, to support them.

How do you think the bank saw this business? The manager really likes this business, as he can be part of a success story. The business is sound and getting better. There is asset cover for the overdraft and the owners' equity of more than twice the bank's exposure. He has a reasonable understanding of the business and has confidence in those people running it – he feels comfortable. He has the opportunity to sell some products and services and knows that if the bank is looking to get rid of managers this customer will not be one that he will lose his job for.

A much happier tale, but what can you draw from this? I think the key points are:

- If you have a corporate manager life can be easier – he or she has more power. However, as a caveat, if you make a corporate manager feel uncomfortable they can descend from a great height – trust me, I have seen it.

- If you are using more than one type of financing it makes your bank feel more comfortable. It shows that you are spreading the risk and that your manager is following others who have decided to back you and your business.

- The bank manager feels he or she knows the business and feels comfortable with it.

- If the economy were to change or the bank decided it needed to pull in its borrowings this business would not pose a problem.

- The overdraft is used occasionally, but each month there is wide fluctuation in cash balances – ie the facility is not 'hard core'.

The contrast between the two businesses and their relationship with their bank could not be more marked. The simple message seems to be that to run an overdraft successfully (ie without grief from the bank manager) you almost have to not need the overdraft facility; you also need to communicate regularly with your bank manager so he or she feels comfortable with you. Bank managers tend to panic and make harsh decisions if they feel threatened.

Term loans

Much of what you have read above holds true for bank loans. They may be dressed up with fancy names such as business development loans, term loans, etc. There are certain similarities to overdrafts except that:

- You make period payments so that the loan (capital) is reduced over the agreed term (three, five, seven years, or whatever).

- It is possible to get 'capital repayment holidays' for the first two years of longer-term loans – which makes them similar in effect to a bank overdraft during this period. Of course this means that the capital repayments have to be spread over the remaining years, which puts up the later years' repayments.

- They can be longer term, to cover asset purchase and large start-up costs.

- Interest is payable but the rate is usually fixed at the start of the loan – this gives certainty to the business on the cost of the loan. The interest paid is an allowable expense against business profits.

- There is an up-front arrangement fee, which again depends on the size of the loan, but no further ongoing costs.

- Once you have agreed a loan from the bank it cannot withdraw it – as long as you are up to date with the payments.

- You will need to put forward your case: how much you need, for what purpose and for how long. A business plan will be required – not just financial projections.

- For most loans the bank will take a legal charge over all or some of your business assets – sufficient to cover the loan if you cannot repay it. If there are insufficient business assets the bank may ask you to give a personal guarantee.

- You can repay the loan earlier than scheduled – usually without any penalty.

Many of my clients have had experience of being forced into bank loans. There have been times when bank managers have tried to convert business overdrafts to term loans – usually in times of concern over the business – as a strategy to reduce their exposure (get their money back). It seems to be a real irony that when a business is struggling to pay its overdraft (which includes no capital repayments) nervous bank managers want to convert some or all of the overdraft into term loans (which do include repayments). I mention this as a word of warning so that you can be aware of your bank manager's next step if you are having grief with your overdraft.

Case study: plastic injection moulding business

Ken Lewis has run a small plastic injection moulding business in Buckingham for many years, which has had to fund the purchase of very expensive equipment (over £150,000 per machine) as well as the working capital needs of a growing business. He has used cheap hire purchase (see later) to fund his machines and an overdraft to fund the day-to-day running of the business. For a couple of years he had marginal profitability with growth. This put him under real pressure from his bank. After some months of exceeding his agreed overdraft facility (together with all the grief that went with it – bounced cheque fees, etc) the bank acted. It sent in investigating accountants, which he had to pay for, and as a result his overdraft was reduced and converted to term loans. This did not help his cash flow any, but it helped the bank – it was going to get its money back over a predictable period – assuming he could stay in business.

As time went on it was clear that the overdraft was not sufficient. With my help Ken managed to secure £100,000 of Business Angel funding (see later). The bank spotted this fresh funding coming in and reduced his overdraft facility by another £50,000 – thereby depriving the business of the additional funding it really needed. I caught up with Ken a few weeks ago – on the day his bank manager was due to visit him. In the two years since I had last seen him, despite difficult times, his debt had fallen quite amazingly. Most of his hire purchase was paid off and some of his bank loans were nearly paid off. The one thing that had remained constant was his overdraft – it was still too small for his business needs. His words to me were, 'If the bank manager pushes me too hard I will change banks', which I think he could now do – his business would be attractive to a new bank manager.

I mention Ken's experience just as a warning – banks will use term loans to give them certainty. In the short term, converting from overdraft to term loan can be painful but if you do survive the transition it can help make your business stronger and debt free.

Small Firm Loan Guarantee Scheme

The Small Firm Loan Guarantee Scheme (SFLGS) is a term loan arranged by all the main banks but guaranteed by the Department of Trade and Industry (DTI). It operates in exactly the same way as a term loan but with some important differences. It is specifically available to most SMEs that have a viable business proposition but which, because they do not have adequate security, are unable to get bank funding. The features of the scheme are:

- In effect the DTI will guarantee to pay the lending bank up to 85 per cent of the outstanding loan if the borrower fails to repay (70 per cent if your business has been trading for less than 2 years).

- Loans are available from £5,000 to £250,000 (up to £100,000 if your business has been trading for less than 2 years) over 2 to 10 years and for most business purposes. Certain types of businesses are excluded according to their size and business activity.

- Loans can be used for any business purpose – working capital, asset purchase, etc.

- Another condition is that the SFLGS must be used to provide additional funding, ie it cannot be used to replace existing funding such as overdrafts, other term loans, etc.

- Arrangement fees are payable and a small premium on the guaranteed part of the loan is payable to the DTI.

- You can choose either a fixed or variable interest rate and make repayments monthly or quarterly. The interest paid is an allowable expense against business profits.

- You do not need to draw down the whole sum borrowed in one go (if you don't need it), which will save you interest charges. However, each tranche must be at least 25 per cent of the total loan and the full loan must be drawn down within two years. Note that this option is only available if you have chosen a variable rate loan.

- Don't forget you will need to submit a business plan – not just financial projections.

Case study: service tents

A friend of mine had invented an innovative tent, which was for use by service engineers. The main advantage was that one person could erect the tent in a couple of minutes around a wide range of working areas. It was a real winner – but he had no more money left. He had poured all his cash into it but needed about another £50,000 to set up proper manufacturing (he was making them in his bedroom) and to market the product. Everyone was convinced that he had a real winner – his customers (who wanted to buy his tents), his competitors (who wanted to buy the rights to his tent), and his bank (who he thought were unfairly financing his main competitor but would not finance him).

   On paper this seemed like an ideal candidate for this scheme – viable business proposition needing more funds but with no security. Did he get a loan? – eventually, but he had to fight tooth and nail. The problem was that this was the early 1990s and the banks were very reluctant to play ball with the DTI over this scheme. The banks, as you will know by now, are in the business of secured lending. In general their rule was, 'No security, no loan'. The SFLGS seemed to them to fly in the face of this principle, even though the government (through the DTI) was guaranteeing 85 per cent of the loan. It was in fact the almost fraudulent benefit that the SFLGS seemed to offer some bank managers that helped its uptake – and helped my friend. He had an overdraft (totally unsecured) of around £20,000, which was making his manager very uncomfortable. At first he did not want to give him any more money until he saw a way of securing his bank's position. If he set up a loan under the SFLGS for £50,000 he could use (improperly) the first £20,000 of this to clear the overdraft (thereby saving his bacon) and use the remaining £30,000 to help the business. In total his exposure was now only £7,500 (15 per cent × £50,000) instead of £20,000 – nice move, and he was seen to be helping his customer.

You may wonder how this loan went through the system. Well, I have to say that it went through all too easily. The system was then (and still is) as follows. All loans under £30,000 under the SFLGS can be authorised by one bank manager – above that it has to go to a second independent manager within the bank. If the second manager accepts the loan application it is passed on to the DTI. Of course the DTI has no real alternative but to accept the loan under the SFLGS – it must assume it is kosher because two independent bank managers have okayed it. As you can imagine, manager one says to manager two, 'I've got a nice little business proposition, will you ok it as it's above my limit? Oh and by the way if you have got any loans you want me to ok for you I will of course help you.' That's how it got through, on a 'if you scratch my back I will scratch yours' basis.

Fortunately times have changed and there is much more acceptance of the SFLGS. All the banks have a lot of experience of doing these loans and probably many have turned out very well. In fact two other friends of mine secured loans under the SFLGS with no problems at all during the late 1990s – but that was after the government put extreme pressure on all the banks to play ball. During 2001 the banks processed record numbers of SFLGS loans – used quite often to help businesses struggling as a result of the foot and mouth disaster.

Before you all rush off to get a loan under the SFLGS let me tell you that it is a one-shot solution, ie if you have one loan under the SFLGS you can not get another (or increase the original). Also remember you are paying a small premium on most of the loan (possibly a couple of per cent) to insure the loan.

European Investment Bank Loan Support Scheme

Some of the clearing banks have been appointed as agents to pass on funds from the European Investment Bank (EIB). The European Investment Bank Loan Support Scheme makes low-cost funds available for capital investment projects that will create new jobs. The EIB is a non-profit-making institution whose shareholders are the member states of the European Union. Loans form £20,000 to £10 million are available over periods of 4 to 15 years, but must not exceed 50 per cent of the total project cost. The interest rate is negotiable.

To qualify, your business should have net fixed assets of under £60 million, and under 500 employees. Preference is given to businesses employing fewer than 250. Your total project expenditure should not exceed £20 million. There is an arrangement fee of 1.25 per cent of the amount being borrowed.

I have little experience of this scheme, but it will help some businesses that are excluded from the Small Firms Loan Guarantee Scheme because they are too big and want too much money. My concern is that limited funds are available and so at times it becomes like a competition, which means that some good business proposals may not get funded – even though they meet the criteria.

Small Firms Training Loan Scheme

All the major banks process these loans on behalf of the Department for Education and Skills. Any business with 50 or fewer employees is eligible to apply. A Small Firms Training Loan (SFTL) can be used to pay for any education or training course and covers course fees, training consultancy or books and materials. Under the scheme you can borrow up to 90 per cent of approved training, subject to a maximum of £125,000. Initially the loan is interest free, with no capital or interest payments for 12 months, depending on the amount you borrow. The repayment period ranges from one to seven years, and a preferential interest rate (variable) will be agreed once repayments start. There is an arrangement fee of 1 per cent.

I have had some clients use this loan scheme to fund their Investors in People programmes and other human resource-related consultancy work.

Hire purchase and leasing

Hire purchase (HP) and leasing are two ways of acquiring long-term assets, such as cars and equipment, when the business does not wish to use a bank overdraft or term loan.

Hire purchase

If you want to own the asset then HP is probably the most attractive option. It is essentially a term loan – usually between two and five years at a fixed rate of interest. The main features are:

- For accounting and tax purposes the asset is treated as yours from day one, and writing down allowances can be set off against your taxable profits. It appears on the balance sheet (as does the loan) and you charge depreciation in your profit and loss account.

- You cannot sell the asset until you have paid off all the HP debt.

- The rate of interest charged is usually noticeably higher than that paid under a personal loan or business loan.

- There are penalties for early repayment (unlike most term loans).

- The assets themselves are the only security the lender (bank or finance house) requires to cover the loan.

- The interest paid is an allowable expense against business profits.

I am sure it is a cultural thing, but many UK business people are hung up on owning things – both personally and from a business point of view. They (and their building society) own their houses and they tend to own most of their large personal assets – cars, TVs, etc. They carry this philosophy over to their businesses. For these people HP and loans are probably the answer to their asset funding needs.

Our European and North American business colleagues are a bit more liberated. Their view, both in business and personally, is that they merely use assets – there is no real need to own them. If you share this viewpoint then leasing/renting (in its many forms) is for you.

Leasing

Essentially, under a leasing agreement you pay (usually monthly) to use an asset for an agreed period of time. At the end of the agreed period you return the asset (in good condition) to its owner – you do not ever acquire ownership of the asset. The main features are:

- For accounting and tax purposes the asset never appears on your balance sheet, and there is no depreciation charge to be made. There is no loan figure to show on your balance sheet. This is what is known as 'off balance sheet' financing.

- You cannot sell the asset because it is not (and never will be) yours.

- The monthly cost is usually less than HP because you are not paying for the whole asset, ie you are only paying for the depreciated value of the asset over the agreed period plus a financing charge. In effect the residual value that the asset has at the end of the agreement goes back to the lessor (owner) and you do not pay for that.

- Usually involves an up-front payment of three months' rental.

- For vehicles there is a restriction on the mileage during the period of the agreement – excess mileage charges apply.

- There are severe penalties for early cancellation of the agreement. In effect you will have to pay the remaining monthly rental charges.

- The whole monthly charge is an allowable expense against business profits. Usually the charge is subject to VAT.

Contract hire

There are of course various twists to the leasing concept, the most popular of which is contract hire. This is used mainly for new motor vehicles. It works very much like conventional leasing (see above for main details) but can involve maintenance, breakdown recovery and road fund licence – basically all you have to do is insure it and put fuel in the vehicle.

Most of my clients use both leasing and contract hire as constituent parts of their financing portfolio. Even as a new business the leasing/contract hire representative has the power to give £25,000 financing to most businesses. Established businesses can get even more. The beauty of leasing and contract hire is that it does not affect your other bank financing – overdraft and loans. In fact your bank will love it because it shows them that you are a sophisticated businessperson who knows how to use a range of financing options.

Key things to remember on funding

Have a funding strategy right from the start

Try to match the funding risk to the business risk. You may find Figure 2.1 helpful in trying to decide whether borrowing (overdrafts, loans, HP, etc) is appropriate to your business. The chart quite simply states that the higher the business risk the less likely it is that debt (bank borrowing) is suitable. Debt is a low funding risk solution only suitable for low business risk situations (eg, taking up a recognised franchise). On the other hand, if you have a high business risk proposition (eg, an Internet dotcom start-up) then it requires a high risk funding solution, such as venture capital.

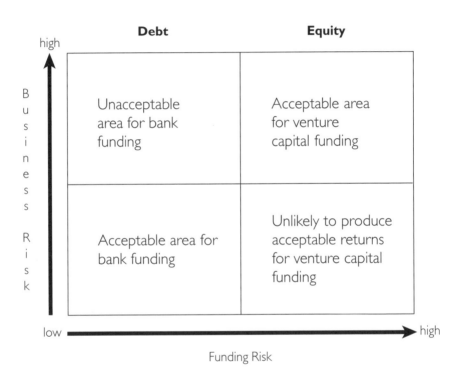

Figure 2.1 Funding and business risks

Match the funding period to the need period

If you want to finance, say, a piece of high-tech computer equipment that has a useful life of only two years, do not be tempted to accept finance over five years. You will end up still paying for an asset long after it has any real use to you. This may seem far-fetched, but there are any number of finance

houses that will let you do this because the monthly payments are cheaper
– typically 50 per cent less each month.

Have a mix of funding products

Don't put all your eggs in one basket. Do you remember my little advertising
agency that needed to buy assets of £35,000, as shown in Table 2.4?

Table 2.4   How assets were financed

Tables and chairs (used)	£1,000	We paid for these
Telephone system (used)	£750	We paid for these
Software (new)	£5,000	2 year lease
Computers, printers, network, etc	£13,250	2 year lease
Working capital	£6,750	Bank overdraft
Working capital	£8,250	We provided this
	£35,000	

In summary, we funded it in three different ways, as shown in Table 2.5.

Table 2.5   How the agency was funded

Bank overdraft	£6,750	(19.29 per cent)
Owners (us)	£10,000	(28.57 per cent)
Leasing company	£18,250	(52.14 per cent)
	£35,000	

This seemed to us a good mix of funding. The bank liked it because it was
in for less than 20 per cent of the risk. It also liked it because it saw that the
leasing company was also backing us for even more of the risk (about 50
per cent) – this meant that other professionals had vetted us and were in for
more than the bank. The leasing company liked it because it was well below

its £25,000 limit for a new business, and it was almost matched by bank and owner equity. All in all, a virtuous circle.

Make sure you can afford the funding with reasonable certainty

Obviously you must check your repayment figures to make sure you can afford them, based on your projected sales/costs. However, as a safety first measure calculate how far your sales could be allowed to drop before you could no longer meet your financing repayments. For example, if your calculation shows that even if your sales were to fall 50 per cent you could still meet the repayments, then in my view this would be an acceptable risk. If, however, a fall of just 10 per cent in sales would wipe out your ability to make the repayments, then in my view this would not be an acceptable risk.

Do not be obsessed with ownership

Do not let your personal prejudices creep into your business decision-making. You may own the house that you live in, but do not feel the need to own the building you trade from, or the vehicles your business uses, or the office equipment it uses, etc. It may be cheaper and less restrictive to hire or lease equipment.

Chapter summary

In this chapter we have looked at the usual range of financing options available to the start-up business. They are of course not exclusively for start-ups – growing businesses will also use these (and a whole lot more options).

3

Growth financing

What is wrong with bank overdrafts?

It is interesting to note that most small and medium-sized UK businesses (SME) use the overdraft as the central plank of both their short and long-term funding strategy. However, they are quite wrong to do so, and in fact European businesses use a far wider range of funding options. The overdraft is appropriate only for financing working capital because it is in theory (and often in practice) repayable on demand.

There is also another downside to the overdraft – it is not very flexible because it is often set at a limit that is not high enough for many growth businesses. Figure 3.1 is a graphical illustration of a high-growth business that needs constantly increasing levels of working capital. As sales grow the need for additional working capital to fund increasing levels of debtors and stock is almost linear, ie if you make an additional £10,000 of sales you may need as much as an additional £5,000 of working capital to fund the stock and debtors associated with this. This ever-increasing need for working capital that is associated with growth businesses and the way it is not well met by the traditional overdraft is highlighted in the figure.

At the start of Period 1 the bank has set a £5,000 overdraft facility. Initially this is adequate, but as sales growth continues the business requires more working capital to support its increasing sales. The area filled in black between the stepped overdraft line and the straight upward working capital requirement line shows the extent to which the business needs more cash than the bank will provide.

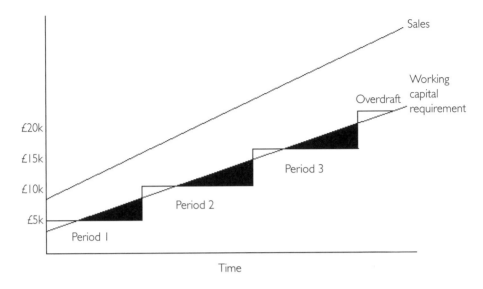

Figure 3.1 The working capital needs of a high-growth business

After some discussion the bank may increase the overdraft facility to £10,000 for Period 2. However, continued sales growth means that the working capital requirement once again breaks through the overdraft facility. The process repeats itself as the bank (this time far more reluctantly) finally agrees to increase the overdraft facility to £15,000 for the start of Period 3. The bank manager can be heard to mutter the words, 'and this time you had better stick within your overdraft'. Unfortunately the rapid growth continues and the business needs more cash. Very soon a £20,000 overdraft is required, which will not be sufficient for very much longer.

This constant back and forth to the bank to 'beg' for additional working capital/overdraft as the business grows cannot be the right way to fund this kind of business. It is expensive because you will be charged an arrangement fee each time, and time-consuming because you will have to put forward a fresh case each time. What the business needs is a stepless funding facility that is constantly right for the turnover of the business. In effect it needs a funding facility the same as its working capital requirement. But does such a facility exist? Yes it does, and it is called 'asset based financing'.

Invoice financing

Invoice financing is a funding facility designed to provide working capital to fund growing amounts of debtors and stock (exactly what the high-growth business typically needs) and only uses these as security for the funding. It can either be provided by your bank or by other specialist banks. It will replace all or most your overdraft, which will mean your bank manager will have to release any other security he or she may be holding, eg fixed and floating charges over debtors and stocks, because he or she is no longer funding them.

The two main types of invoice financing are factoring and invoice discounting, and stock finance. Factoring and invoice discounting are similar in effect and enable the business to access up to 90 per cent (usually) of the sales invoice value of the goods sold, typically within 24 hours. This means a business always has the level of funding it needs for the level of sales it is currently achieving. The remaining 10 per cent (less charges) is paid over when your customer pays. Stock finance, in combination with the above, can make up to 100 per cent of the sales invoice value available almost immediately. This type of arrangement can be very useful to businesses with seasonal demands.

For both of these, annual fees based on sales value are charged and vary according to the level of service bought, which can be very comprehensive. Interest is payable on the money borrowed at a rate that is usually slightly cheaper than bank borrowing. There are subtle differences between factoring and invoice discounting and, depending on your business requirement, one or both may be appropriate.

Factoring

Using this the business 'sells' its invoices to a factor (usually part of a bank) and contracts its sales ledger administration to the factor. This can include full bad debt protection (called 'non-recourse factoring') or exclude bad debt cover ('recourse factoring'). The former is more expensive because it covers an element of bad debt insurance, so that the factor cannot have any comeback (recourse) against the business if the debt goes bad. It is usually available for businesses achieving or forecasting turnover of around £50,000 plus per annum.

Invoice discounting

Using this the business exchanges sales invoices for cash but retains full control over its own invoicing and debtor collection. Bad debt protection can be provided as part of this package. Invoice discounting will usually be the cheaper form of debtor financing if no other service is being used. It is usually available for businesses achieving or forecasting turnover of around £750,000 plus (with no upper limit).

Stock finance

Using this the business makes its stock available as part of an 'all-inclusive deal' with either or both of the above to increase the amount of cash available against its sales invoices. This is in effect the sweetener to uplift the 90 per cent advance to 100 per cent of sales. This form of financing is particularly suitable for manufacturing businesses that have to buy in stock and process it over, say, several weeks to generate sales. With this type of facility financing becomes available to buy in stock as well as fund debtors. The main banks will not touch this with a barge pole because they have got their fingers burnt before, but there are some specialist banks that will provide this form of financing.

Case study: Dairyborn

Dairyborn has become a very successful cheese business and in recent years was sold for in excess of £20 million. However, I remember doing some work for its MD, Robert Segesser, when cash was tight. A feature of his business was that the product, cheese, was a relatively simple one and was rarely the cause of disputes with his customers. What was an issue was that his customers were taking between 60 and 90 days to pay. As the business grew its sales from £1 million towards £20 million cash became a real problem. His bank did not feel comfortable with providing ever-increasing amounts of overdraft, but suggested they switched to invoice discounting or factoring. They chose invoice discounting because they already had a pretty efficient accounts department – getting invoices out and collected was not an issue, so why pay someone else to do this? The problem was entirely due to the speed of growth putting constant pressure on the overdraft.

How did things work out in practice? In general there were a few changes that had to be made. The only change to the invoicing procedure was that they had to raise an additional copy of the invoice and send that to the bank, which would then release 80 per cent of the invoice value within seven days (this was a long time ago and these percentages and times have changed now). This meant that in the first month of going onto invoice discounting there was a sizeable increase in the effective bank funding. Table 3.1 shows how sizeable this can be.

Table 3.1   Aged debtors

Total	Current	30 days	60 days	90 days	120 days +
380,000	200,000	100,000	50,000	20,000	10,000

Bank overdraft	50% current to 90 days		185,000
Confidential discounting	80% current to 90 days		296,000
Extra (one off) injection of cash by discounting			111,000

In this example we see that the bank would typically advance up to 50 per cent (as overdraft facility) against what it calls good debtors – those less than 90 days old. In this case it would advance £185,000 against book debts of £370,000. However, when this business switches to confidential discounting the amount advanced by the bank increases to £296,000 (80 per cent of good debtors less than 90 days old). This represents a one-off increase in bank funding of £111,000, which is by anyone's standards a very worthwhile improvement.

In addition they had to send signed copy delivery notes to the bank – why? Well, if they were advancing money on the sale of cheese they wanted to make sure that the cheese was actually being delivered. There have been many instances of businesses (not this one I might add) issuing phoney invoices for fictitious goods just to get the 80 per cent advance of cash. If the delivery notes did not arrive within seven days then the bank would claw back the cash advanced on these sales.

Another twist was that the bank wanted to see the monthly aged debtor report – why? Because they would claw back any cash advanced against sales that were not paid within 90 days. In a bad month when customers were disputing deliveries and delaying paying on other invoices, the overall working capital funding was quite severely reduced. For the accounts department, monthly bank reconciliations also became a bit more complicated.

The final twist was that as long as sales continued then the funding from the bank was ever increasing. But what would happen if sales were to take a nosedive? Fortunately this did not happen to Dairyborn, but it would have meant that the banking facility would in effect decrease; this is shown in Table 3.2.

Table 3.2 The effect of increasing sales on the banking facility

	Jan	Feb	Mar	April	May
Monthly sales	200,000	150,000	100,000	50,000	40,000
Maximum monthly advance	160,000	120,000	80,000	40,000	30,000
Loan facility 296,000	440,000	520,000	520,000	400,000	270,000

In this example we see that after the £296,000 advance, sales start to decline from £200,000 per month to £40,000 per month. During January to March the actual loan facility increases – despite sales going down. This gives the business a buffer of help during the period that sales start to decline. However, as the sales slide continues during April and May the loan facility very quickly falls to £270,000 – a reduction of over £250,000 from its peak of £520,000. The problem is that in May the business will still need the higher level of financing, but unfortunately is severely restricted in the cash available. As I said before, fortunately this did not happen to Dairyborn – but it could happen to you.

As we can see, confidential discounting worked pretty well for a growth business like Dairyborn. It enabled it to have an adequate loan facility that grew with sales. A real bonus was that the improved loan facility meant it always had cash available to use to improve the business. Occasionally it had the opportunity to buy cheese offered by suppliers at a discount – but only if it bought large quantities. It had the cash to do this and this typically enabled it to improve gross margin by several per cent. It also enabled it to optimise production because it had cash available to fund bigger production runs for increasing sales. In the old days it was rather stop-start as it struggled to pay suppliers.

All in all, a success story for this company, but how long do companies typically continue to use invoice financing? Well, not forever. Typically they drop this kind of financing at turnovers of around £10 million per annum. Recent surveys have shown that only some 3 per cent of businesses above this size are using it – beyond this level they have either generated their own cash reserves or have access to better bank borrowing facilities.

In the past factoring had a bad name because business people usually assumed that if a business was factoring it had cash flow problems and was one step away from going bust. This was probably an unjust criticism of factoring, which has now matured and has offered discounting (which is confidential) and does away with this problem – a business's customers do not know that it has financed its debts.

Asset-based financing has come of age and is now accounting for somewhere in the region of £70 billion of working capital funding in the UK alone. On this basis it cannot be ignored.

Should you use invoice financing?

Confidential discounting costs in the region of 1 to 2 per cent of all turnover plus the cost of the money being borrowed. Factoring will cost between 2 and 5 per cent of all turnover plus the cost of the money being borrowed. It costs more because they are doing more for you – in effect they are your accounts and credit control department. Assuming current bank base rates of around 4.25 per cent (May 2004) then to a reasonable risk business this will cost 7 per cent to borrow. Add to this the cost of factoring and the total cost is 12 per cent of sales (I know it is a rather crude measure). If you have a gross profit of 15 per cent then you have only about 3 per cent to cover all your other business costs. Invoice financing is only really applicable to those businesses that have really good gross profit margins – typically 40 per cent plus.

What do you do if your gross margin is very small, say less than 10 per cent? Well, for a start you can't use factoring but confidential discounting may work for you. However, some types of business will not qualify for confidential discounting – namely those that do not have a tangible product. If you sell widgets then invoice financing may be available. If you sell airline tickets, as many travel agents do, then invoice financing will not be available – and the low margin really precludes this. What should you use? The choice is probably a bank overdraft together with credit card sales – you make your customers pay you by Amex or Visa in full each month. This costs about 2 per cent but guarantees immediate payment. Also, if you are really clever you add a surcharge for payment by credit card.

Chapter summary

In this chapter we have looked at invoice financing as an alternative to a bank overdraft. This is available from all the banks, although stock financing is only available from some specialist banks. In many respects invoice financing is the ideal form of growth financing for fast growth businesses. Its pros and cons are as follows:

- Pros:
  - flexibility: funding is always available in line with the level of sales, without preset limits;
  - improved cash flow helps the business plan better and obtain better deals from its suppliers;
  - can be used either short or long term;
  - factoring can in some cases be better and cheaper for a business than running its own credit control department.
- Cons:
  - external third party credit control when using factoring (may upset some of your customers);
  - cost, because fees are based on sales value;
  - some types of business may not be acceptable.

4

Equity funding

Giving money away

In the previous two chapters we have looked at borrowing money – either for working capital or asset purchase. These have their limitations, which have already been outlined. As we know, all banks are in the business of secured lending – but where do we go if we have a risky project that the banks will not touch? Suppose you have a project that needs £1 million to make it happen. Chances are that the banks will not touch it – especially if you are a new or small business. The answer may be to take on an equity partner. In effect you sell some of your business to one or more people. This can work in all sorts of ways, depending on how much money you need to raise. You can do this by either offering shares to the whole wide world (usually by what is known as an initial public offering or IPO) or by offering shares privately to just a handful of investors (commonly referred to as a private placing). Which of these methods you should use will for the most part depend on how much money you want to raise. Either way you raise money without borrowing – so there are no interest costs and you don't need to pay the money back.

If this sounds interesting, then read on.

Let's start with the more modest ways of raising equity (or risk) financing, although the principles for most forms of private placings are very similar.

Business Angels

Business Angels are usually high-worth individuals who make equity (shares purchase) investments in businesses. Quite frequently, as well as money they can bring valuable skills and contacts to a business. They will typically commit amounts of between £10,000 and £100,000 to a single business. Where a larger sum is required they will often work in a syndicate with others. Business Angels are usually serial investors and will make more than one investment each year and over several years. They will invest in businesses at any stage of their life but tend to support at an early stage – start-up or early expansion. They are catholic in their tastes – they will invest in most business sectors. They are, however, quite parochial and will usually invest in businesses close to where they live or work.

They operate quite informally, either on their own or through Business Angel networks. In most respects they operate in the same way as venture capital firms – investments are made primarily for financial gain. However, quite frequently they will have more than one reason for investing in a business, which may well work to the advantage of the business receiving the investment. They may want to play an active role (part time) in the business in which they are investing. This gives them the chance to use their business skills for the benefit of both parties. A further benefit is that as business people they may be able to bring useful contacts to fit the business.

The key factors that they take into account are those that any venture capitalist would regard as important. In addition there are other considerations that are specific to Business Angels:

- They may be prepared to accept lower returns than a venture capitalist if there is an opportunity to be involved.

- They will always be minority shareholders so they are not a threat to the current control of the business.

- They are likely to be able to make quick investment decisions (quicker than a venture capitalist), which will save time and money during the process.

- They are prepared to make longer-term investments but will seek similar exit routes as a venture capitalist.

- They are unlikely to make more than one investment in a business due to their more limited funds.

Unfortunately, Business Angels want to remain anonymous so you will not find them in *Yellow Pages* – this stops them from being swamped with proposals. This means that they can only be found through Business Angel networks, which act as introduction services. Fortunately, these networks are quite visible and there are over 40 listed in the *BVCA Sources of Business Angel Capital,* which gives a profile of each together with contact details.

You will find that your local Business Link is also a good starting point to contact Business Angels. They will often arrange 'beauty parades', whereby businesses wanting funding have a chance to present their business proposition to a panel of Business Angels.

Case study: Ken Lewis Engineering

Ken Lewis runs Ken Lewis Engineering and for several years it had endured a poor relationship with its bank (I would like to say who it is but the legal ramifications could be severe). The business reached a point at which it needed additional cash, which the bank would not provide. Together we calculated that the business needed around £100,000 to secure its short to medium-term future. Fortunately, Ken knew someone who could easily be described as a 'high worth individual' – he just happened to be a director of a prominent auction house. I suggested that we approach him with a proposition.

The proposal was that for £100,000 he would receive 10 per cent of the ordinary shares in the business, thereby valuing the business at £1 million. New shares would be issued so that the acquirer could obtain Enterprise Investment Scheme (EIS) relief. I guess it might be helpful to just mention a bit about the EIS at this stage. The EIS replaced the Business Expansion Scheme in 1994 and offers tax incentives to individuals who invest in the ordinary shares of certain types of high-risk, unquoted trading companies. Attractive tax benefits apply once the shares have been held for three years – essentially you can sell them and not pay any capital gains tax as long as you have held them for the full five years. You can also receive dividends (although these are taxable) but this does not affect the favourable capital gains treatment. Most trading companies qualify for the EIS and a business can raise up to £1 million a year this way.

Doing the deal was simplicity itself. I drew up a simple two-page document that set out the terms of the deal. It included a brief section on the company's dividend policy, stating at what levels of profit what dividends would be triggered (and how much). How has it worked out for both sides? Ken got the money that he desperately needed so his business has continued. Currently he is being courted by an acquirer who wants 100 per cent of the business. The previous Business Angel deal has set a marker down in the sand – he is expecting to achieve £1 million times the percentage improvement in the business since then. How did it work for the investor? Well, you must not forget his investment of £100,000 really only cost him £60,000 – the nice people at the Inland Revenue gave him a cheque back for £40,000 (EIS tax relief). In addition he has received dividends and, if the business is finally sold for in excess of £1 million, he will get back at least £100,000.

In Ken's case the Business Angel only provided money – he did not get involved in the business nor did he interfere in any way.

Venture capital

There are organisations that specialise in funding business propositions that have risk. These are venture capitalists and over the last 30 years they have become the main source of risk capital in the UK. Their primary means of supporting businesses is through the provision of equity funding, ie they buy shares in the company which they are supporting. However, some of them can act as banks as well – so you can get the best of both worlds.

The important thing to recognise is that equity funding is quite different to bank funding. Banks make loans and are repaid capital and interest according to an agreed schedule. They can lend to any type of business organisation – sole traders, partnerships or limited companies. Venture capitalists give money to a business in exchange for pieces of paper, called share certificates. They are buying a share of the company and so do not have such a clearly defined route for the return of their money. Their expectation is that at some time in the future the business will pay dividends and that their investment will grow in value. They will only get their money back when someone else buys either their shares or the whole company's shares. Equity funding is only available to limited companies.

The starting point is to find a venture capital provider and to do this you will need a business plan. This will detail your business proposition, the funding you require, how and when it is required, financial projections, and details of the business's performance to date. To help you find the right venture capital provider you will need to be specific about the stage of funding and industry sector.

Stage of funding

Venture capital providers do not fund every stage of business development and each has its own preferences. The recognised stages for funding are:

- Start-up: financing for product development and early marketing. At this stage the product has not been sold commercially.

- Other early stage: financing for commercial manufacturing and sales. At this stage the company will not have generated any profit.

- Expansion financing: as its name implies, this is financing to increase production, marketing, product development or additional working capital for established businesses. It can also include recovery funding and refinancing of bank debt.

- Secondary purchase: buying existing shares from another venture capital provider or other shareholders.

- Management buy-out (MBO): funding the purchase of a company by the current management team.

- Management buy-in (MBI): funding the purchase of a company by an outside management team.

- Institutional buy-out (IBO): funding the purchase of a company by a venture capital provider prior to the management team (either existing or new) acquiring a stake in the company.

- Leveraged build-up (LBU): where a venture capital provider buys a company with the purpose of making further acquisitions to create a larger business group.

Industry sector

By the same reasoning each venture capital provider has its own sector preferences and will generally not make investments outside of these. The common sectors are: agriculture, biotechnology, chemical and material, communications, computer related, consumer related, construction and property, energy, environmental, financial services, food, industrial automation, industrial products and services, leisure, media, medical/health related, other electronics related, other manufacturing, retail, transportation, and investment outside the UK.

Having identified and approached an appropriate venture capital provider, who will be interested in your industry sector and stage of funding, the next step is to negotiate and conclude the deal. While this is a simplification of a process that will involve lawyers, accountants and considerable time and money, it is essentially the rest of the process. At the end of this process you will have agreed:

- a valuation for your business;
- the amount of funding you will receive;
- what share of your business the venture capitalist will acquire in return for their money;
- the terms of the deal (contract) incorporating how the business will be managed and controlled;
- an outline exit route and timescale.

Fortunately it is considerably easier to find a venture capital provider than a Business Angel since they are actively looking for business proposals. All the reputable venture capital providers belong to the British Venture Capital Association (BVCA), which provides a directory of UK-based venture capital providers. This has a profile on each one, covering such details as:

- address, telephone number, e-mail and Web site address;
- size – people and money invested;
- where they get their money from;
- how many companies they have invested in;
- minimum and maximum investment amounts;
- stage and industry preferences;
- geographical preferences;
- who to contact.

Before you make any formal approach it is recommended that you talk to your financial adviser and make sure your business plan is up to scratch.

Valuing a business for venture capital

Let me say something up front. While valuing a business is a well-trodden process, there will be times when a business will be worth more (or less) than the underlying financial projections. This may be due to the venture capitalist or Business Angel wanting to do the deal with you because they want your type of business in their portfolio. On the other hand, if they have already invested in too many businesses like yours (sector/size) that year they will try and give you a rotten deal to drive you away. Do make sure that you are prepared to stand up for yourself. Of course I can't give away all my valuation secrets: I would get thrown out of the magic circle. However, I can tell you the basic rules, which are incredibly simple.

Assuming that the investor is interested in your business then the following are the key factors taken into account in valuing a business:

- *The perceived risk* – if this is a new business with no track record, unproven management and a new product/service, then this will attract a high-risk rating. On the other hand, if the business and management have a track record and the product/service is already recognised (it is just doing it quicker/better/cheaper/faster) then this will be seen as having very little risk. This factor may be used to adjust the required rate of return or downgrade the future value of the business.

- *Your customer base* – if the business plan shows a good spread of customers with none accounting for, say, more than 10 per cent of your sales, then this will be favoured. On the other hand if the business has a small customer base it will be seen as very vulnerable and this will concern an investor. This factor may be used to adjust the required rate of return or downgrade the future value of the business.

- *Maintainable profits* – this is key to the valuation of a business. An investor will value a business on what they believe its future maintainable post-tax profits will be. Of course it is quite likely that the year three profits are projected to be higher that year one – that's ok but an investor will discount profit forecasts further than one year ahead so it may not be advantageous to base a valuation on, say, year three profit forecasts.

- *Required rate of return* – this will obviously affect valuation. Let's say that a risk-free investment (eg, a building society) is yielding 5 per cent. An investor may want 20 per cent per year, which equates to a return of 2.5 times their original investment over five years, for a low risk investment. On the other hand, this same investor may want 40 per cent per year, which equates to a return of 5.4 times their original investment over five years, for a higher risk investment. You may think this is greedy, but if they make higher risk investments then the chances are that out of, say, every 10 investments, 6 will go bust – so the remaining 4 have to make a higher return to get an acceptable result overall.

- *Industry price/earnings (P/E) ratio* – the final consideration must be how many years' worth of profits the investor is paying for to arrive at the future value for the business. If you have, say, an engineering business making £50,000 per annum (and capable of making it for many more years) would you be prepared to sell it for £50,000 (one year's worth of earnings)? Of course not. So how many years' worth of profits should an investor pay for?

For more traditional businesses where maximum profitability is being achieved now (like engineering) the P/E ratio (or profit multiple) is likely to be low – say 3 to 6 times. That means that an investor will pay 3 to 6 times the annual maintainable profits to arrive at the future value of this business.

On the other hand, where the business is in a new and innovative sector (Internet-based businesses are a good example of this) where maximum profitability is not being achieved, the P/E ratio may be as high as 20 or 30 times – because the investor is expecting better to come.

The choice of P/E ratio will have a profound effect on the future value of the business. It is not correct to look in *The Financial Times* and take an average P/E from there because these businesses are quoted (and therefore have a larger market for the shares) and bigger (and therefore a lower risk). The correct approach is to look for similar businesses that have been sold recently (this may come from talking to an experienced intermediary) and adopting a similar P/E.

The final part of the equation, which does not affect the valuation but does affect how much equity an investor will receive, is the amount of money you need. For example, if a business is valued at £150,000 and the owners want to raise £50,000, an investor will get 33.33 per cent of the equity (£50,000/£150,000).

Case study: Beechwood Enterprises

Beechwood Enterprises Limited has been trading for one year as metal finishers, with an inexperienced management team. To fund its next stage of growth it has decided to raise £150,000 by means of an equity investment. Its projections are as shown in Table 4.1.

Table 4.1   Beechwood's projections

	Turnover	Profit before tax
Current Year	£375,000	£37,500
Year 1	£500,000	£62,500
Year 2	£662,000	£75,000
Year 3	£850,000	£112,500

Let's assume that a P/E ratio of 6 times has been agreed and that the investor is looking for a 35 per cent return because they perceive the business to be high risk. How then should we value this business?

Stage 1

What is the future value (FV) of the business?
    Using the formula: FV = maintainable profits × P/E value:

Year 1   Profit £62,500 × 6 (P/E) = £375,000 future value
Year 2   Profit £75,000 × 6 (P/E) = £450,000 future value
Year 3   Profit £112,500 × 6 (P/E) = £675,000 future value

On the face of it things look straightforward – we should choose the year that yields the highest value, which is year three profits. Because this is two years away our investor will discount this by 35 per cent for each year away. So let's look at these three years again applying this factor and using the following formula:

Present value (PV) = Future value (FV)

$$(1 + i)^n$$

Where: i = Investor's required rate of return, n = Number of years until forecast profits.

Year 1: PV $\dfrac{375,000}{(1 + 0.35)^1}$ = $\dfrac{375,000}{1.35}$ = £277,777

Year 2: PV = $\dfrac{450,000}{(1 + 0.35)^2}$ = $\dfrac{450,000}{1.8225}$ = £246,913

Year 3: PV = $\dfrac{675,000}{(1 + 0.35)^3}$ = $\dfrac{675,000}{2.460375}$ = £274,348

On this basis it clearly makes sense to use year one forecast profits because this yields a present value of £277,777. The other years yield lower present value because of the discount factor being used.

Stage 2

How much equity will the investor acquire?

The final stage is quite straightforward and calculates how much equity they will get for their £150,000. Having established that the business is worth £277,777, then £150,000 buys £150,000/£277,777 = 54 per cent of the equity.

As a final note on valuations, the same process is used for Business Angel valuations – but it is usually slightly simplified. However, the Business Angel investor is usually acquiring a minority share and consequently the valuing process is a bit more informal and they would buy at a higher price than a venture capitalist.

Alternative Investment Market (AIM)

AIM is the London Stock Exchange's public market for small, young and growing companies, wherever in the world they are based. It allows businesses to raise capital (sell shares) by means of less arduous entry criteria and with a less stringent regulatory regime than a full Stock Exchange listing. Entry to AIM allows a company's shares to be traded on a public market. Since its start in June 1995 (as a replacement for the Unlisted Securities Market or USM) and up to 31 January 2002 there have been a total of 1,018 admissions to AIM, which between them have raised just over £7.3 billion. Today these businesses have a market capitalization (value) of £11.2 billion. Table 4.2 gives some interesting statistics on the growth over the last seven plus years of the AIM.

If we accept that AIM is an important way of bringing equity funding to small, young and growing businesses, what do we need to know? Let's see if we can answer some questions about AIM.

Why join a public market?

- To provide access to capital for growth – that's probably what most people are initially interested in.

- To create a market for your company's shares – giving a readily accessible way for existing shareholders to exit the business (and withdraw full value).

- To obtain an objective market value for your company – provided daily as a result of investors being able to buy and sell shares and that information being available to the public.

- To encourage employee commitment – by making share schemes more attractive and thus capable of acting as an incentive for employees' long-term motivation.

- To increase the company's ability to make acquisitions – using quoted shares as currency (instead of money).

- To increase the public profile of the company – press coverage, analysts' reports.

- To enhance status with customers and suppliers – who are reassured by the discipline imposed by a regulatory body like the London Stock Exchange.

Table 4.2 Growth of the AIM, 1995–2002

	Number of companies			Market value (£m)	Number of admissions			Money raised £m		
	UK	International	Total		UK	International	Total	New	Further	Total
June 1995	10	0	10	82.2						
1995	118	3	121	2,382.4	120	3	123	69.5	25.3	94.8
1996	235	17	252	5,298.5	131	14	145	514.1	302.3	816.4
1997	286	22	308	5,655.1	100	7	107	344.1	350.2	694.3
1998	291	21	312	4,437.9	68	7	75	267.5	290.1	557.6
1999	325	22	347	13,468.5	96	6	102	333.7	599.8	933.5
2000	493	31	524	14,935.2	265	12	277	1,754.1	1,319.7	3,073.8
2001	587	42	629	11,607.2	162	15	177	593.1	535.3	1,128.4
2002 to Jan	593	41	634	11,229.8	12	0	12	11.5	32.6	44.1
Launches to date					**954**	**64**	**1,018**	**3,887.6**	**3,455.3**	**7,342.9**

Source: London Stock Exchange

Why join AIM?

- Easier entry criteria – available to a wide range of companies giving them access to a public market at an earlier stage of their development. No trading record is required (new companies are ok), no pre-set levels of profit are required, and any percentage of shares can be in public hands.

- A less stringent regulatory regime – permits a company to be a public company without the full disciplines of the UK Listing Authority's rules.

- Tax benefits – investors can enjoy EIS, Venture Capital Trust, Corporate Venturing Scheme, CGT holdover and taper relief.

- Easier acquisition rules – making growth through acquisition much easier.

Who can join AIM and who do you need to help you?

- Virtually any business can join – new or old.

- Appoint a nominated adviser (NOMAD) who will judge whether your company is appropriate for the market, explain the AIM rules to you and, after admission to AIM, will ensure you comply with the rules.

- Appoint a broker (this could be your nominated adviser) who will help bring buyers and sellers of your shares together both before and after the flotation. Post-flotation they will act as market makers for your company shares to try and ensure liquidity, ie a plentiful supply of shares available to buy and sell.

- Appoint a legal adviser who will oversee such issues as directors' contracts and verification of the statements in your prospectus/ placing document.

- Appoint reporting accountants (this could be your auditors) to conduct an independent review of your company's financial record.

- Appoint investor relations advisers (a PR company) to manage the flow of information to potential shareholders during the flotation and existing shareholders post-flotation.

What specifically do you need to do to join AIM?

- Appoint a nominated adviser (NOMAD).

- Prepare an admission document (also known as a prospectus/placing document) – this contains all the relevant information investors might need on your company and its activities, including financial information and projections. Your company's directors are responsible for the accuracy of this document – both words and figures within it and those omitted, if material. The Exchange also requires information on major shareholders, the past records of all directors, and a statement of working capital adequacy.

- Appoint a broker.

- Place no restrictions on the free transferability of shares – this will involve changing the company's articles and memorandum.

- Pay an annual flat rate fee – to continue membership of AIM.

What is the final timetable and documents required?

- Ten days before share float, make an announcement to the market of intention to float.

- At least three days before share float, make an application to the Exchange supported by the following documents:

  - admission document;

  - application form signed by the directors;

  - declaration signed by the nominated adviser;

  - a letter from your company's broker confirming its appointment.

● Additional information required:

- full details of the directors: previous directorships within the last five years, unspent convictions for serious offences, and all bankruptcies, receiverships or liquidations;

- details of any shareholders entitled to control 3 per cent or more of the votes at a company general meeting;

- working capital report: a report produced by your company's reporting accountants to state that there is sufficient working capital to meet current requirements;

- details of any party that has received £10,000 or more in fees, shares or benefits from your company in the 12 months up to admission.

What does it cost to join AIM?

As you can imagine, the whole process of getting ready to join AIM is an expensive exercise – the lawyers, accountants, NOMAD, etc can cost an arm and a leg! Then on top of all that there is the fee for being admitted to AIM.

The admission fee

Think of it as an exclusive club membership. The amount of the fee depends on how much money you have raised. The latest fee costs (as from April 2002) are shown in Table 4.3.

It's probably best to show how this works with an example. Suppose your business has just raised some cash on AIM and has a market capitalisation (ie the total number of shares in existence times the float share price) of £7 million. Locate this value in the appropriate band column (a) – it falls in the 5 to 10 band. Then multiply the amount by which £7 million is over the value of the 'greater than' figure (£2 – forget about the millions) by the corresponding figure in column (b) (£500). This gives a value of £1,000 (£2 x £500), which you add to the maximum fee of the previous market capitalisation band (£5,000). In this case a company with a market capitalisation will pay £6,000 (£1,000 + £5,000) as its admission fee to AIM. So far so good?

Table 4.3 AIM fee costs (from April 2002)

(a) Market capitalisation (£m)		(b) Increment per £ million	Maximum increment £	(c) Maximum fee £
greater than	less than			
	5	fixed fee	–	5,000
5	10	500	2,500	7,500
10	50	250	10,000	17,500
50	250	125	25,000	42,500
250		55	7,500	50,000

Annual fees

After admission to this exclusive club you have to pay each year to retain membership. Again the fees payable are based on market capitalisation (overall value of the business) as at 30 November prior to the 1 April following (annual fees run from 1 April to 31 March). Minimum annual fees are £5,000 (for companies up to £350 million capitalisation) and maximum £20,000 (for companies over £350 million). Companies above £350 million capitalisation pay an additional £7.50 per million above this figure. Fees are pro rata (on a daily basis) for new applicants' joining data up to the following 31 March. Fees are invoiced annually in advance on 1 April. Note that for companies joining after 30 November the actual market capitalisation at the time of admission is used for calculating the fee.

Cost of raising money on AIM

So far we have seen the smallest part of the cost of getting on to AIM – the bulk of the cost is incurred by paying all the advisers, accountants, lawyers, brokers, NOMAD, etc. As a guide the all-inclusive cost of raising around £2 million on AIM is about £250,000.

Case study: raising money on the AIM

A company I know raised £10 million a few years ago (if I mentioned the name I could not give you these details). It was quoted a cost of £750,000 (excluding VAT) in total to achieve this. You can imagine the surprise the company had when actual costs came in at £950,000 (including VAT). The company had done everything it could to save costs by combining the role of NOMAD and broker; it used a provincial solicitor to carry out some of the routine legal work (property title confirmation). It still needed top-notch lawyers (to protect the directors) and also had to pay for the top-notch lawyers used by the investors. Along the way it paid for specialist PR to make the right splash and a top-six firm of accountants to do the accounting reporting. Mark, the MD of the company raising the money, said that suddenly all sorts of costs arose that he had never envisaged.

His advice to anyone thinking of raising money on AIM is to:

- Be thorough with the quotations from the various parties needed. Get them to include typical costs – not the bare minimum (which never happens).

- Also question every bill you are not happy with – believe it or not everything is negotiable, especially when they want paying.

- Get as many people as possible to act on a no float, no fee basis – you may be surprised how many advisers will act in this way. In Mark's case the company's stockbrokers were prepared to do so.

- Shop around – there are plenty of people out there who can do the job. Do not fall into the trap of letting one adviser nominate another, thus making sure that all their cronies get a slice of the action. Always act on personal recommendation, if at all possible.

Costs

Below is a brief insight into how the costs broke down to raise £10 million on AIM.

Stockbrokers
They charged a retainer of £25,000, which was all they would get if the full money were not raised. In addition they charged a corporate adviser's fee of £200,000 and a sliding scale commission for successfully raising the money – 2.5 per cent on the first £9 million raised, and 1.25 per cent on the

next £1 million. Their commission came to £237,500 all told. Finally, for good measure, nearly £5,000 of 'out of pocket' expenses mysteriously appeared. All in all it cost just under £500,000 in stockbroker fees.

Accountants
The company used one firm of accountants (a top-six firm) to do all the accounting/tax/share structure work. They charged £105,000 as a retainer, £15,000 for the audit, nearly £30,000 for tax work, and around £25,000 to tidy up old and new share option schemes. There was even a fee to convert the company to plc status and yet again 'out of pocket expenses' reared its ugly head – just under £1,500 in this case. In total, accountancy work cost around £195,000.

Lawyers
Here is the real sting – the company had to pay not just for its own lawyers' costs but just about everyone else's involved in the process. Lawyers' fees amounted to around £100,000. 'Out of pocket' expenses amounted to around £9,000 – it transpired that many of the long meetings at their offices involved breakfasts, lunches, dinners, etc, and the lawyers charged for these. All in all the lawyers cost around £145,000.

Property valuations
Between the solicitors and property valuations another £30,000 was spent. Yes, once again 'out of pocket' expenses appeared, but only about £500.

Public Relations (PR)
Just one firm was involved in spreading the word. This cost nearly £40,000. This included £7,000 of 'out of pocket' expenses.

Printing
Of course a glossy prospectus was prepared, closely proofread, and sent out to a handful of people. This cost £16,000.

Sundry items
There were other costs involved in getting the job done. Temporary accounting staff were required to prepare the necessary financial information. This cost around £20,000. Specialist insurances cost £26,500 – these

cover the directors for their personal liability if anyone makes a claim against them for misleading any investors. In total these cost around £35,000.

This is not an exhaustive list but it does give a good flavour. Just a couple of final points. *VAT:* most of these costs include the dreaded VAT – as a final insult, not all of this can be reclaimed. *Corporation tax:* while many of these costs are allowable for tax purposes, quite a lot are not. I remember having to pay a tax/VAT specialist to help me through this minefield.

Timetable and effort

So far we have looked at the reasons for joining AIM and the costs, but what are the timetable and effort required? From my own and Mark's experience it is a thoroughly traumatic time. Remember that you have a business to run and yet the accountants, lawyers, etc want another 150 per cent of your attention. At the same time you have a target date by which you want to float. This may not seem too critical – what is a week or two among friends? Well, timing is critical. When my company floated on AIM in 1998 we set a very tight timetable – less than three months. We hit it to within the day, but if we had missed it by just two weeks we would have failed to raise the money we needed. Why? There was a complete change in market confidence – our sector had suddenly fallen out of favour. Let me highlight a typical timetable; Mark's is shown in Table 4.4.

The whole process lasted just over three months – and during that time it is sheer manic activity, with one meeting after another. Let me just pick out a couple of examples.

Verification meeting

Imagine a room full of people round a large table. Typically there will be at least two to three lawyers, two to three accountants, your stockbroker's representatives, your NOMAD, and finally a couple of secretaries taking notes. In addition there should be all of your company's board of directors – if they are not all there it will involve additional phone calls.

So what is the purpose of this august meeting? It is to verify every word in your prospectus or placing document as being truthful. Imagine the situation. Each of you has a draft of the document in front of you. As a board you will be asked to provide proof that every statement in the document is

Table 4.4   Outline flotation timetable

End of November	• Appoint sponsor and broker
	• Preliminary valuation work undertaken by sponsor
	• Other advisers selected
	• Engagement letters circulated
	• All parties meeting
	• Timetable agreed by all parties
	• Engagement letters signed
December	• Work commences on:
	– long form report, accountants' report, working capital report and profit forecast (by accountants)
	– legal due diligence report (by lawyers)
	• Outline listing particulars drafted
	• Personal tax planning considered
	• Float vehicle determined (Newco?)
	• Tax clearances submitted to Inland Revenue
January	• Reports reviewed by company and sponsor
	• Drafting of listing particulars continues
	• Litmus tests with institutional investors
	• Listing particulars submitted to Stock Exchange for review (at least 20 clear business days prior to publication)
	• Research note published
February	• Verification of listing particulars undertaken (overseen by lawyers)
	• Reports finalised
	• Marketing presentation finalised
	• Marketing to institutional investors (one-to-one meetings and/or larger presentations
End February	• Listing particulars finalised
	• Pricing of new shares
	• Completion meeting (board approves flotation)
	• EGM
	• IMPACT DAY (ie listing particulars approved by Stock Exchange and published, and application for admission to Official List made)
Approx one week later	• Admission to Official List effective and dealings in shares commence
	• Cash received from investors

true and the evidence of such. This will eliminate statements such as, 'XYZ Ltd is a fast-growing software company' – how do you prove the words 'fast-growing'? Out go the words 'fast-growing'. Then you have got to prove the word 'software' – hopefully a bit easier, this one.

When I attended our verification meeting it took a whole day and was driven (brilliantly I may add) by our lawyers. During the day there were a number of side meetings between various parties to agree differences. I seem to recall that as our company was concerned with software, year 2000 compliance was a real issue – but sensible negotiation won the day. You have to remember that everyone in that room wants the deal to happen – they are all just trying to protect their rear ends. A few meetings like this and you are exhausted. You also start to understand where all the 'out of pocket' expenses start to appear – 15-plus people round a table all eating, drinking, phoning, faxing and e-mailing.

Marketing to institutional investors

As a board you have the job of persuading institutional investors to invest. Your stockbroker will set up the meetings but you have to do the persuading. This means endless meetings with 'poker-faced' hardened investors who have 101 other things they need to be doing. The schedule below is how just one of Mark's days looked – and remember there were five like this:

Thursday 17 February
  9.15   Singer & Friedlander
10.30   Newtons
11.30   AIB
12.30   Lunch, Mercury
14.30   SG Asset Management
15.45   Phillip & Drew

Fortunately much of this was done in London, but imagine flying up to Scotland as well! Also, you must be very careful during your presentation. You will be asked weasel questions like, 'What do you think your profits will be next financial year?' Stick to the script and be non-committal about the future.

I hope I have given you a reasonable flavour of AIM. It has helped many companies to raise growth money. It can also be used to release cash to exiting investors, although typically they will be 'locked in' for 12–24 months. However, it has not worked for all companies. There has been an argument that AIM does not offer very much liquidity for shares, ie there is not a very active market for their shares. Also, it is claimed that any sales of shares have to be channelled through the company's stockbroker, which acts as a further control on prices/activity. This may be true, but AIM does work for truly successful growth companies and can be viewed as a stopping-off point before an eventual full listing.

I will leave you with this thought. You will always get a better price for your business by selling shares on AIM rather than to a venture capitalist – typically you will get two to three times the price. Does this help make the pain more acceptable?

Stock Exchange (full or main listing)

Much of what you have read about AIM also holds true for a full Stock Exchange listing. To achieve a full listing is the ultimate goal of some businesses. The reality is that very few businesses either try to or achieve this status. Achieving a full listing is even more expensive and rigorous. It would be outside the scope of this book to deal in any detail with this area.

Should you use equity funding?

To be honest, equity funding is only for the small elite of businesses. From an investor's point of view it is totally unsecured and highly risky. If things go wrong you can't ask for your money back. This means, for it to be an attractive proposition, your business must be highly desirable, which means that it must have demonstrated historical growth in sales and profitability over the last three to five years in excess of 30 per cent per annum. Only this level of growth gives your investor the level of return they need.

As well as historic financial performance and anticipated future performance, your business needs to have an ambitious growth plan to be right for equity funding. If your strategy includes launching new products, moving into new markets, acquiring other competing/strategic businesses, etc, then this will make equity funding appropriate. If your strategy includes more modest growth, doing a bit more of the same things, then equity funding is not for you – it would make more sense to use bank funding, HP, leasing, etc.

Chapter summary

In this chapter we have looked at equity funding – Business Angels, venture capital, AIM. All of these involve selling some part of the business. There are common benefits and pitfalls to all of these:

- Pros:
    - you are not borrowing any money, so there are no ongoing interest costs and capital repayments;
    - you can bring in large amounts of money, typically far higher than banks will lend;
    - Business Angel funding can be done quickly and quite cheaply with little investor interference;
    - Venture capital and AIM funding can be used as a step up to raise further funding as the business grows/wants to acquire other businesses;
    - AIM: your company shares have a recognised value (it's shown in the papers every day), which makes it easier to buy and sell shares, to release value or raise additional cash. You also get the best price for your shares.
- Cons:
    - AIM is costly and time-consuming;
    - Venture capital: poor price often offered for shares;
    - selling equity involves parting with some ownership of the business: some people have a real problem with this;
    - AIM and venture capital are really only appropriate for fast growth, higher than average profit generating companies.

5   *Buying a business*

Why should you buy a business?

I suppose that any business looking for accelerated growth is entitled to consider all the options. If that business is profitable and cash rich (or has access to funding) then there are two recognised methods of achieving this.

First, there is growing your own business, otherwise known as 'organic growth', where a business concentrates all its resources on growing its own core business. This can be achieved by doing more of the same or diversification. Second, there is growing through acquisition, which in effect is recognising that organic growth is not possible or will not happen quickly enough. This can involve acquiring a similar business (doing what yours does); a complementary business (fits in below or above yours – vertical integration); or a different type of business (diversification).

The temptation for those people who believe that organic growth is not happening fast enough or will not enable the business to meet its profit objectives, is to acquire another. Let's have a look at the two options to see their comparative virtues.

Organic growth

- Risk

    - Business risk: without doubt the low-risk option. If you attempt growth through selling more of the same product to similar customers then there is virtually no business risk at all. If, however, you attempt to grow by diversification, ie selling totally new products to totally different customers, I would suggest that this is a high-risk activity. This is in effect a new business, using some existing resources but bringing in other new resources.

– Funding risk: if the growth is within the same market place (customers and products) then the funding risk is low: you are just buying a bit more of what you are already buying. Your only concern would be cash flow. If the growth is through diversification (new customers and new products) then this is a medium to high funding risk – you will be hiring new people, developing and making unfamiliar products. This will involve the large-scale purchase of assets.

● Cost – organic growth is usually less costly than acquisition. Scaling up in a business can cost only a few thousand pounds. Much of the cost is marginal – a bit more of this and a bit more of that. If the growth is through diversification then the costs can be more substantial but still only in tens of thousands of pounds.

● Return – scaling up offers very high returns because of the low cost and high returns. Diversification can be quite disappointing and offer lower returns than the core business.

● Speed – most organic growth is relatively slow to yield substantial growth, especially if the business is mature. In newer, more dynamic businesses, where core sales growth is faster, the organic growth is faster but still not capable of doubling turnover in, say, three years. Diversification can be painfully slow.

● Ease – most organic growth is reasonably easy to achieve, especially if you are using the same people and resources. Diversification is more difficult, especially since management typically underestimates the task.

Growth through acquisition

- Risk

  - Business risk: potentially very high risk in the case of diversification or vertical integration. The limited knowledge of customers, products, workforce, management, finances, etc of the business being acquired compound this business risk. However, the acquisition of a similar business to your existing business is a medium business risk activity, if done in a professional manner. It could be argued that this option is no more risky than organic diversification.

  - Funding risk: if the growth is through diversification or vertical integration then the funding risk is very high, but it can be reduced depending on how much of the purchase price is for goodwill (to buy the business – high risk) and how much to buy assets (low risk). If the business being acquired is a clone of your existing business then this is a medium funding risk.

- Cost – undoubtedly the costly option. First, there are the professional fees, which will cost several thousands of pounds. Then there is the cost of the business, which is based on a multiple of profits plus the cost of any assets acquired. Overall it may cost two to three times more to acquire a business than to achieve the same growth organically.

- Return – has the potential to yield very high returns if you buy at the right price and integrate the two businesses successfully.

- Speed – acquisition offers a quick growth option, which cannot be matched by organic growth. Particularly useful if there is a 'window of opportunity' that must be seized – in most cases organic growth will miss the boat. Can provide a business with a way of doubling sales almost overnight.

- Ease – extremely difficult to integrate a newly acquired business due to cultural differences, location, potential management indifference/ work overload, and stress on systems.

How do you buy a business?

Later on in this book we will look at grooming a business for sale and then selling it, but for now you are on the receiving end of the selling process. Hopefully by the time you have read this section and the later sections you should be fully wise on how to buy and sell businesses. For the time being let's look at the stages involved in finding and buying a business.

Before we start to look at these aspects in detail I must pass on to you the observations of other business people I have known who have bought and sold businesses. The consensus seems to be that the more times you do it the better you get at it. What this does tend to suggest is that if you only ever buy one business you are unlikely to get it completely right – you might pay too much, pick a poor business, or fail to integrate it with yours. It seems that over time as you buy businesses you refine your approach and tend to get all these aspects right eventually. From my own experience, I know that you have to look at a lot of businesses before you find one that is worth making an offer for.

Finding a suitable business

You will find businesses for sale in a wide range of daily and weekly publications. These range from *Daltons* and *Exchange and Mart,* which are good for retail businesses, to the broadsheets such as the *Telegraph, The Times* and *Financial Times,* which are good for manufacturing and service businesses. In addition you will find trade-specific publications that include adverts for businesses for sale. You will also find businesses for sale via the Internet. While I am sure that these all serve some purpose I am not quite convinced that this is how I would try to find a business that I wanted to buy – it's a bit hit and miss and very time-consuming for potentially very little reward.

My preferred option would be to choose a trusted or recommended intermediary. This could be your accountant or solicitor, or someone who they or a trusted business friend might suggest. This way you are dealing with one person who knows what you are looking for, has a reputation to protect, and will only put forward to you businesses that they know to be worthwhile. In effect a lot of the filtering has been done for you. The end result is, hopefully, one or more businesses that you want to find out more about.

Establishing how good it is

Assuming you know something about the market in which the prospective acquisition operates, you need to find out how good a buy the business may be. You will find that most serious sellers of businesses have already put together a basic seller's pack. This will usually be a one or two-page overview. It will not state the business name but it will give some basic data such as turnover, gross margin, pre-tax profit, number of employees, facilities, business type, geographic location (but probably not town), reason for sale, and asking price. If this still interests you and you want to know more you will have to approach the person or organisation shown in the details you have received.

You will usually find that you are dealing with either a firm of accountants or a selling agent. In either case they will want to check out how serious (and knowledgeable) you are before they will send you anything. Ideally they want to be dealing with principals (the buyer) or their professional advisers. Before they will send you any further information, they will ask you to sign a confidentiality agreement. This is a legally binding document under which you agree not to disclose any of the confidential information you will receive to any other party without authority. You can understand the seller's position – they don't want to be giving out their secrets to their competitors or any other nosey individuals.

Do bear in mind that what you are going to receive is information that shows the business in its most positive light. There will not be any lies but there may be omissions. If I were buying a business I would want to know the following:

- Historical financial performance – certainly at least the last two years' detailed profit and loss statements and balance sheets. In addition I would want to see at least the last five years' figures summarised: turnover, gross profit, net profit, etc.

- Current year budget and performance to date – this would let me know how well the business is currently performing and what it expects to do for the remainder of the financial year.

- Statement of resources – this would let me know what facilities it has (offices and production capacity/equipment) and how good these are (age and specification). It should also include a full breakdown of the workforce: age, skills, what they currently do in the business, length of service with business, salary, etc. I know it may sound heartless, but if you are going to buy a business there is a strong possibility that some people may have to be made redundant, so having this information will help you work out how much it will cost you.

- Products or services – this should include specification sheets and brochures, if they exist. Also, it should provide details of how long these products or services have been offered and what changes have been made over the years (and any proposed) so you can form a view on how good they are.

- Customer base – this will be a touchy area so be prepared for a total lack of names of customers. However, the company should be able to tell you how much the major customers bought over, say, the last two years and how many customers it has and their average turnover. You will also want to know about any contractual arrangements the business may have with any of it customers.

- Order book – this is a vital health indicator. If the business has no order book then you are buying nothing other than the possibility of selling to previous customers. If the business has a six-month order book then you have at least some firm future.

- Contingencies – you will want to know about anything nasty that might be about to crawl out of the woodwork. Are any suppliers threatening or obtained judgements against the business for non-payment? Does the bank (or anyone else) have a charge over any of the assets – particularly fixed assets, stock and debtors? Will they release these when you acquire the business? Do any customers have claims against the business for faulty goods? Are their any bad debts? These are just some of the main questions you may want answers to. You will want the seller to warrant these – assure you in writing that what they are saying is the truth.

- Competitor/market analysis – it would be nice to think that this was available for the business that you are thinking of buying, but it probably will not. So ask the sellers who their competitors are and how big they think their market is.

Armed with this information you can start to form a view of how good the business appears to be. You should be able to eliminate the real no-hopers at this stage. Hopefully you will see something in the business that makes you feel that you have found a genuine one with some real potential. The next stage is to work out how much it is worth to you.

Deciding how much it is worth to you

Needless to say you must work out what the business you want to buy is worth to you, which is not necessarily the same as what the seller wants (usually lower). I would, however, suggest that you pay particular attention to your evaluation of maintainable profits. As a result of your calculations you will arrive at what the business is worth to you. For further help, refer to the section on venture capital in the previous chapter, which will refresh your memory on how to value a business.

What if the business is not profitable – what should you pay for it?

Negotiating with the seller and doing the deal

If your valuation of the business and the seller's are the same then a deal will be quickly struck. However, the reality is that you will value the business somewhat lower than the seller will. Suppose that you valued the business at £1 million and the seller thinks it is worth £2 million, then the difference in expectations is probably too much for a deal to be done. You might put the offer in writing (subject to plenty of legal get-out clauses) and see what happens. You are likely to follow it up with a phone call to discuss it further but it will probably be rejected.

Let's suppose that your valuation of the business is £1.75 million and the seller wants £2 million, then I would suggest that since the difference is only 12.5 per cent a deal could be struck. Do remember that both buyer and seller each have their own highest and lowest price respectively. If the seller needs £2 million to provide for their retirement then that has to be met somehow. It may be possible to meet this requirement by some clever payment arrangement. If, however, the seller needs £2 million to buy another business then there may not be any scope to come down from this figure without involving a third party. Find out why the buyer has set their selling price and how critical it is to their other plans. If the price is set in stone then you will need to find some area to negotiate on if you still want the business.

The selling price may only be one part of the deal that you both need to feel comfortable with. The other considerations for both parties, which will need to be dealt with, are the following.

Basis and timing of payment

After agreement has been reached on the selling price then payment could be due in one of several ways. If you have had to pay top value for the business then it should be possible to negotiate stage payments, eg 25 per cent on completion with the remaining 75 per cent payable in instalments. This could be based on business performance, eg if the business achieves agreed turnover and net profit figures during the next year, then the remaining purchase price would be payable. Alternatively the remaining price could be paid over an agreed period of time, say in six monthly instalments.

If some form of stage or conditional payment has been agreed then the seller will want some security to cover this. First, they will have a contract, which lays down the agreed basis. To give them extra comfort the remaining equity (over and above the initial 25 per cent paid for) could be subject to either a 'right to purchase' or a 'lien or legal charge'. In other words you as the purchaser have a contractual right and obligation to buy the remaining 75 per cent (right to purchase). Alternatively, you as the buyer acquire all the equity but until you pay for the remaining 75 per cent the seller retains voting control and can seize these shares back until they are paid for.

The assets to be included

Regardless of whether the asking price is paid or not there is always scope for some of the assets to be excluded from the deal. In fact as buyer you should be very careful to ensure that you are acquiring ownership of everything you think you are entitled to. Do check ownership of every key operational asset to make sure that it will become yours or that the lease can be passed on to you. If a business operates from freehold premises and these are a substantial part of the purchase price, you may not want to take this on – either because you want to relocate the business or have a policy of renting assets to maintain flexibility. It may be possible to agree not to buy, or let the seller be your landlord. This is frequently done – the bank will always lend against freehold property with a tenant.

Tie-in of owner-manager

During the first 6 to 12 months it is absolutely critical that the new business performs to expectations. Most small businesses are still very dependent on their owner-manager, so during this critical period you may want to keep them on board until you can really get to grips with the business. It is usual practice to tie in the owner-manager in one of two ways. First, they can be given an employment contract for, say, two years. This keeps them within the business and legally prevents them from setting up in competition to you. You keep them for however long you need them, which is typically 12 months, and then pay them off for the rest of the contract. Alternatively you can put them on 'gardening leave' whereby you pay them but they stay at home. Once again this prevents them from setting up in competition to you.

The second, and least favoured option is to try and construct a 'no competition' clause in the purchase contract. In other words you take the view that you have no use for them within the business after you buy it but you do not want them setting up in competition straight away against you. In effect you need a head start. My own experience is that these sorts of contracts are doomed to failure. Ideally, you would want a clause that prevents the seller from setting up in a similar business in your geographic area within, say, 12 months. Such a contract would probably fail at law because it would be deemed to be unfair restraint of trade – you can't prevent a person from carrying out their own trade.

To tie in the owner-manager that you are buying from you really need some leverage. The best leverage is to ensure that some significant element of the purchase price remains unpaid for a period of 12 months. This way it is in their own best interest to ensure that they do what you want them to. It is not uncommon to insert into the purchase contract a bonus (or ratchet) agreement that incentivises them to perform.

Securing the customer base

I don't want to sound too alarming, but the customer base is absolutely vital to the future of the business. If it walks with the seller then you have real problems. Ensure that all key accounts are tied into the business. If there are no contracts then either get some in quick or look at some other way of securing the customer base. In most service type businesses it is not uncommon to have contracts. If, however, you cannot tie in the customers with a watertight contract then isolate them from the seller in some way.

When I ran an advertising agency I had a policy of what I called 'three points of contact' with every client. The purpose of this was to ensure that the client knew they were dealing with a larger professional organisation behind the account handler that they had day-to-day contact with. Every three months each client would receive a 'courtesy' visit from me to make sure that everything was ok – it also gave me a chance to sell to them. At the same time I made sure the creative director (who I trusted implicitly) also contacted them on a regular basis. That way we hoped that our clients would feel as if they were part of a bigger family – they knew at least three people within our business. We also made sure that we knew and had contact with more than one person within their business. Of course the proof of the pudding is in the eating – or testing in our case. One of our account handlers left and tried to take their key accounts with them. I made some phone calls and visited the clients involved to fly the flag and reinforce how dealing with us would be better than dealing with a freelance. Fortunately, we kept all the key accounts.

In summary I would say that you must do your best to secure the customer base. Contracts can work but if a customer wants to leave they will and there is very little you can do to stop them. If there is financial loss as a result of a breach of contract then you should negotiate a settlement – try and avoid going to court because nobody really wins.

Securing the key staff
The last thing you need is for the key staff to walk as soon as you buy the business. This could happen for a whole raft of reasons. When it becomes public knowledge that you are going to buy the business you should interview all the key staff to find out what their concerns may be. There will probably be uncertainty and a feeling of loyalty to the departing owner-manager. They will want reassurance that they are not going to lose their jobs. It is possible that they do not have formal contracts of employment, in which case a good move would be to offer them contracts that give both parties security. If key staff are planning to leave then try and identify them early so you can respond quickly to limit the damage.

Securing the funding

I know this may sound stupid but do not leave this vital stage till last. The sensible thing is to talk to your financial backers (assuming you need financial help) before you start to look for a business to buy. The chances are that a variety of longer-term funding will be required so you might need the support of more than one party – we have covered most of these earlier in this book. At the minimum you will need a business plan that shows your business and the business you are buying and how they will improve as a result of the acquisition. In fact, regardless of whether or not you need outside funding, you should prepare a business plan for the enlarged business just to make sure it makes the sense you think it does.

You should aim to get yourself into a position where you have negotiated the funding and have a letter of intent. Make sure potential funders are aware of the likely timescales involved so that when you need the money it is available. Do remember that as well as the purchase price you will need additional working capital. You will be surprised how many times I have seen people buy a business and then struggle because the increased debtors and stock are way beyond their current banking facilities.

Integrating the new business

Assuming that you have an existing business that you want to integrate with the new business, you must consider this at the time of negotiation.

Case study: acquiring a software company

Some years ago I was tasked with negotiating a deal to acquire a software company on the southeast coast for a business based in Buckinghamshire. My chairman had met up with our stockbrokers and they had agreed that a marriage between the two businesses made sense. There would be no problem in getting the money to buy out the business, subject to my finalising the deal. I met their managing director and finance director, who came armed with hundreds of business plans, financial projections and annual accounts. We did talk numbers but my most immediate concern was how the two businesses could be integrated.

I had serious reservations about the roles for some of their board members; for a start we did not need two finance directors! Also, I had concerns about managing a bigger business that was spread out over two sites some 100 miles apart – we found it difficult enough to manage and control one office. My final concern was over the two different cultures within the businesses. We were more formal and structured, whereas they were very laid back with an apparent lack of management. After some deliberation I felt that we would probably fail to integrate the two businesses. We certainly could not relocate their business so there would always be some element of 'us and them'. In the end I had to recommend to the board that we did not buy.

I guess the moral of my story is that you cannot just weld two businesses together and expect it to work. If you want synergy then there needs to be some strong element of compatibility and a well thought out plan as to how this will be achieved. It is hard work!

How do you make sure there are no nasty surprises afterwards?

You should not take at face value any information you are given by the seller. To further improve your chances and reduce the possibility of your being sold a pup there are some additional things you should do:

- obtain a warranty from the seller that all critical facts are correct;
- obtain a third-party verification of all assets and liabilities (balance sheet audit);
- obtain a third-party verification of any financial forecasts;
- obtain the best tax and legal advice you can afford;
- run your proposed acquisition past as many people as possible to get their feedback.

If you have done this and your proposed acquisition gets the thumbs up then you can be as sure as possible that you have done all the right things. Let's have a look at each of these in just a little detail so that you know what to look out for.

Warranties

A warranty can be defined as a statement made in a contract, which if unfulfilled does not usually invalidate the contract but could lead to the payment of damages. If the warranty is clearly stated in writing it is known as an 'express warranty', and if it is not but is understood by both parties it is known as an 'implied warranty'. So how do you as the buyer make use of this? The answer is to make sure that you question every statement of fact and ignore every statement of opinion. So if the seller makes any statement that is important and that may influence your decision to buy, ask them to provide the proof to back up it up, and if there is still any uncertainty ask them to provide a warranty in the sale contract. The warranty should be given by the directors of the company (in the case of a limited company) or by the proprietor or partners (in the case of an unincorporated business).

How might this work in practice? You are buying a business but are uneasy about the level of returned goods and other outstanding claims that customers may have against the business. Your big concern is that a major customer may have a valid but as yet undisclosed or known action against the business. Potentially this could lead to non-payment of a large sum of money and a claim for damages for consequential loss. If this situation were to materialise the business would be worth considerably less than the current price.

Under these circumstances you need a warranty in writing within the sale contract. In essence this will state that the directors warrant that there are no outstanding actions either already commenced or about to be commenced for faulty or non-delivered goods and any consequential liability caused by this. The warranty would be valid for, say, two years. Should any of the stated events occur then you have the comfort of knowing that you will be able to claim damages for the effect of this on the business.

As a final option you may want a small part of the purchase price to be held back from the seller until the warranty period has expired. Normally this would not be an acceptable course of action but if there are some very real concerns (based on previous experience) then holding back, say, 10 per cent of the purchase price will give you some extra comfort.

Balance sheet audit

While the seller will provide historic financial information in the form of audited accounts and management accounts there will be a gap between audited figures and the current position. The concern must be that in the period, say six months, since the last audited balance sheet, things might have changed. For example, assets may have been sold, levels of debtor are not as high (or as sound) as stated, levels of creditors are higher than stated, and so on. You need confirmation of the state of play today. The way that you achieve this is to employ an independent accountant (your auditor will do it) to carry out a balance sheet audit.

The balance sheet audit will systematically construct and verify the balance sheet for the business you are buying. This will be done from the records that the business has. In addition your accountant will seek third-party verification of the figures. For example, let's say the business has debtors of £200,000. By any account this is a very significant asset and you would want to make sure that this value was correct and that it was all fairly current and collectable. Your accountant will take the debtor list, if there is one, or create one if there isn't. Then the accountant will write to a selection of these debtors (debtor circulation) to ask them to confirm how much they owe the business and the age of this debt. The business will send out the debtor circulation letter (on its headed notepaper) authorising the debtor to return the information required directly to your accountant.

A similar approach will be taken to other critical figures within the balance sheet – bank balance, hire purchase, trade creditors, etc. As a result of the balance sheet audit you should feel very confident in the figures you now have. Of course, if the negotiations go on for some time the value of this activity may diminish because some months may pass by. You should leave this activity as late as possible. If there is a gap between the balance sheet audit date and the final date of completion, ask the directors to warrant the changes.

Verify the financial forecasts

It is quite possible that the sellers of the business you are interested have prepared budget figures, which they have shown you. Obviously they are telling you that this is their view of how the business is going to perform over the next 12 months. There is a strong chance that you may be influenced by these figures, especially if they are designed to make you believe that the business is going to grow sales and profits substantially. I guess I would equate this to a used car salesman saying to you, about the car you are interested in, 'It's a lovely little runner, three careful owners, only done 45,000 miles and does 50 miles to the gallon.' I think I would want to see some proof of this and I might want a mechanic to check out the condition of the car.

So how do you check out any profit and cash flow forecasts that you are shown? Once again I would enlist the support of an independent accountant (your accountant). They have the skills to verify the forecasts – in fact they could do it at the same time as they are doing the balance sheet audit. In essence they will audit the forecasts to check that:

- the calculations are correct – its quite amazing how many errors there are in spreadsheet projections;

- the basis on which assumptions have been made are correct – eg if the cash flow shows that debtors pay in 30 days, a check is made to verify that in the past debtors have paid in 30 days. If historically they have paid in 60 days, then the cash flow is going to be too optimistic;

- the sales growth is realistic – no one can guarantee sales growth but it is possible to state whether the projected sales growth has any semblance of reality. This will be done by looking at historic growth, eg if in the past average sales growth has been 10 per cent per annum and the sales projections show 30 per cent for this year then my immediate thought would be 'no way'.

The objective of verifying the financial projections is to increase the level of confidence in the financial prospects of the business.

Take tax and legal advice

I suspect that your knowledge of tax and law is somewhere between 'not a lot' and 'even less than not a lot'. I am a chartered accountant with a reasonable working knowledge of most business-related accounting, finance, tax and law, but I would always take advice if I were spending large amounts of money. There are pitfalls at every corner when buying a business. I think you will agree that the contract itself, together with any warranties, needs the skills of a good commercial solicitor. It is a specialist job, so don't see the solicitor who did the conveyancing on your house. You will pay considerably more for a commercial solicitor but they have done what you require hundreds of times before, so they know all the wheezes. If you use a good solicitor then you should not go too far wrong.

You may wonder why you need tax advice if you are buying a business. You certainly need it if you are selling a business – to make sure that you end up with more of the sales proceeds than the taxman does. However, even buying a business can be a tax minefield, especially if you are buying a business from a sole trader or partnership. The main issues are:

- Past tax history of the business – have all the taxes been paid and are there any outstanding Inland Revenue enquiries? Is anything going to crawl out of the woodwork and bite you? With a limited company, payment of tax is relatively straightforward – the company pays it. With sole traders and partnerships it is significantly more complicated because the business does not pay the tax – the individuals do and there may be little proof of this.

- Current year's tax computation – has this been correctly calculated and agreed with the Inland Revenue?

- Tax losses – if you are buying a business with tax losses, are these transferable to your business?

In addition there may be PAYE issues that need clarifying. For instance, a friend of mine ran a business in which they used about 50 self-employed sales people. They did this because it made it easier to get rid of them and also it saved on NI contributions and was easier to administer. They also did not deduct tax from their payments. The Inland Revenue had constantly challenged this arrangement on the basis that these sales people were really employees and as such PAYE and NI should be liable. There was also the threat that had any of these sales people not paid their tax, the company would be liable for its payment. The feeling was that some day the Inland Revenue would have its way and a large tax bill would land on the company's doorstep.

Using professionals in an area that you have little knowledge of is only common sense. The cost will be far outweighed by the benefit.

Get others you trust to check out your plan

I am really suggesting that you get opinions from as many people as you can. The reasoning behind this is that if more than one person views the proposition, any glaring faults in your reasoning will be spotted. Don't get them to look at the technical stuff (contract, audited accounts) unless they ask and have knowledge of these areas. Ask them for their opinion/comments on the overall idea of buying this business (or even any business). You may be surprised at the very practical comments that they will make.

Ask your wife or another female what she thinks of the idea. I am a great believer in women's intuition. They are great at judging people. My ex-wife was extremely perceptive and would often comment to me, on meeting someone for the first time, 'I don't trust him – be careful.' On every occasion she was correct. The problem is that you are always too close to the situation and want it to be right.

Talk to any business colleagues you have to see if they have bought a business before to find out what pitfalls they encountered. My own experience is that buying a business is a risky and difficult process and if you can get input from as many people as possible you will minimise the chances of failure. My own view is that you improve with experience at buying businesses.

Should you be buying a business?

It all depends on your business objectives. If you have a business that is profitable with good cash flow and growing at above 20 per cent per annum then stick with organic growth – you should not be considering acquisition. If your business has slowed down, but is cash rich (or has access to funds) then acquisition can revitalise this type of business, especially if it buys in better management with the business it is acquiring. The final consideration must be timescale. If your market is changing and your size of business is under threat then acquisition may be the only way to survive – organic growth will not provide survival.

So, now you are clear on your motivation for wanting to buy a business, but can you handle it? You need:

- a strong business to start off with – profitable, well managed and with access to financial backing;

- a positive vision of how the new business will fit into the new family and the determination to make that happen;

- the support of the business that you have acquired.

Chapter summary

Buying a business is a nightmare (not dissimilar to the nightmare of selling a business that I outlined under AIM in the previous chapter). To do it successfully you must minimise the variables. You do this by surrounding yourself with trusted advisers and not taking at face value anything the seller shows you or tells you. The benefits and pitfalls of buying a business are:

- Pros:
  - can be the quickest and cheapest way to give a boost an under-performing business: just witness the takeover activities in the financial press;
  - can provide you with the opportunity to take out painful/ annoying competitors;
  - can be a way of buying in a better management team: the one that comes with the business you are buying.
- Cons:
  - very difficult to get right: about 75 per cent go wrong for various reasons: wrong price, wrong business, failure to integrate, wrong funding;
  - not always cheaper than organic growth.

6

Debt-bound and failing businesses

Never give up

It would be nice to have a book that talks only about success – unfortunately that is not reality. If I am really honest I have seen as many business failures as I have seen those that have sold for millions of pounds. However, failing businesses have value. The task is to protect that value, improve it if you can, and then when you can do no more, find some other party to buy the business from you for a value in excess of what it is worth in your hands. While it is beyond the scope of this book to go into great detail on improving a failing business, I will just visit the headline activities that you should concentrate on (you will find much more detail in my book *The Bottom Line;* see the Sources of help section).

Restoring some profitability and managing cash

The important thing is to remember that if cash is tight, do not try and grow the business – this ruins weak businesses because it puts too much pressure on working capital. The key is to make much more profit out of every £ of existing sales you have coming in. The main areas to focus on are the following.

Improving gross margin

Improving gross margin must be the number one activity. The key messages are: increase selling prices; change suppliers/renegotiate supplier terms (downwards); change your product/service specification (to reduce cost); improve buying (shop around); and rationalise labour (lay off/consolidate rates of pay).

Reduce overheads

You can use most of the measures highlighted above to reduce overhead costs. The important thing is to concentrate effort where there is the greatest potential for payback. It's the old 80/20 rule – in this case 80 per cent of the savings can come from 20 per cent of the overhead categories. If your overheads cost £1,000,000 a year do not waste your efforts on some cost category that costs only £5,000 a year (0.5 per cent of the total cost). Look for a category that costs, say, £50,000 a year – a saving of 10 per cent will yield £5,000 (not just £500 as in the other cost category). You can cut out a lot of expense before service levels fall – just look at what the banks have done in recent years by getting rid of thousands of employees. Do things differently. A business I know decided that by converting all their newer petrol vehicles to LPG they could reduce their fuel costs from around 80p per litre to 40p per litre.

Chase debtors hard

Small businesses do not like chasing money – ask any bank manager and they will confirm this. The problem seems to be that they always see debtors as customers and not as 'villains' who are holding on to cash that is rightfully theirs. To be successful you must depersonalise debt collection. The key messages are: send your invoices out earlier, find out how your customers payments systems work (to make sure you are complying), chase debtors earlier (even before they become overdue), and have a system (don't just chase debtors when you are short of cash).

Control stocks

The sole purpose in buying and making stock is to sell it on, as quickly as possible and for the highest price. On this basis stock holding should be kept to a minimum. It is, however, a balance between having sufficient to meet customer demand and having so much that it becomes obsolete and of no value. The key messages are: link stock levels to sales, and identify slow/obsolete stock and get rid of it (to raise some cash).

What will it do for your business?

This will depend on how bad things are to start with and how much effort you put in. Even a small improvement in all the areas shown above will make a big improvement when consolidated in a business. In the example shown in Table 6.1 we can see how just a 5 per cent improvement in these areas has led to a 145 per cent [(£39,200 - £16,000)/£16,000] improvement in net profit. It has also led to a significant improvement in working capital due to reduced debtor and stock funding – down from 40 per cent of turnover (£96,000) to 36 per cent of turnover (£90,720) – a saving of £5,280.

Table 6.1 Effect of 5% change on key areas

	Before	**After**
Sales	£240,000	£252,000
Cost of sales	£144,000	£136,800
Gross margin	£96,000	£115,200
Overheads	£80,000	£76,000
Net profit	£16,000	£39,200
Debtors	£60,000	£57,000
Stock	£36,000	£34,200
Debtors + Stock %	40	36

Based on this example it must make sense to work on margins, overheads, debtors and stocks.

Selling an unprofitable business

You may reach a point at which you decide (or it is decided for you) that it does not make sense to continue owning/running the business. Quite simply you cannot add any more value, either as a result of your management/leadership, chronic under-funding, or inherent lack of profitability. The temptation is to unload your business at net asset value, because that's all you think it is worth. Wrong – your business is worth far more than that. In much the same way that a profitable business may be worth less than the owner believes (because a buyer does not view it so optimistically), a loss-making business can be worth far more than the owner believes (because buyers can see what they can do with it). How then do you make your loss-making business into a must-have business for someone else? Your business is attractive to someone else with a similar business who wants to:

- grow turnover to achieve a bigger presence in the market – people start to take you seriously;

- improve buying power with key suppliers – suppliers start to be keen for your business and offer discounts;

- make cost savings and improve the profitability of both businesses – shared administration costs, shared management, shared premises, etc;

- share expertise to grow both businesses faster;

- remove a competitor who may be driving down prices and hence reducing profitability;

- make an existing business bigger and more profitable, ready for sale to a trade buyer.

There are as you can see many good reasons for acquiring a loss-making business, and I am sure you can think of some more.

How much will they pay?

The answer is – how much is it worth to you? You must look at what you can do with the business to see how you can either make it profitable or how it could be used to improve the combined businesses.

Case study: selling a printing business

Mark Johnson wanted to sell his printing business which last year on a turnover of £1 million made a net loss of £40,000. I suggested that if we could find the right buyer he could get as much as £1 million for his business – even though the business had no significant net assets. There was a brief period of incredulity (I think his words were something like, 'If you can do that you're a miracle worker'). Fortunately the business was stable even though it was making a loss. I produced a short information memorandum, which focused very heavily on the benefits (cost savings/market share, etc) that might accrue to a competitor if they were to acquire the business. The proposition was that this was a golden opportunity to buy a business that could be bolted onto another similar business very easily to improve both businesses. Last year's profit and loss statement for the business being sold is shown in Table 6.2.

Table 6.2 Last year's profit and loss statement

Sales		£1,000,000
Cost of sales (materials)	60%	£600,000
Gross margin		£400,000
Overheads:		
Administration		£75,000
Management		£150,000
Directors		£150,000
Rent, rates, etc		£50,000
Depreciation		£15,000
		£440,000
Net profit		−£40,000

The seller has suggested that a buyer, with a similar business that offers similar products to the one being sold and shares many customers, could make immediate cost savings. Below is a summary of the changes we suggested could be made within three months and the benefits the new combined business would achieve:

- Combined purchasing of materials would reduce cost from 60 per cent of sales to 55 per cent for both businesses.

- By combining sales of both products, selling prices could be increased by 5 per cent due to the reduction in competition.

- Administration staff costs could be reduced by £25,000 per annum (one person) with a redundancy cost of £3,000.

- Management staff costs could be reduced by £75,000 per annum (two people) with a redundancy cost of £10,000.

- The co-director of the acquired business (the owner-manager's partner) would not need to be employed in the new business. This would save £75,000 per annum but cost £25,000 in redundancy costs.

- There is room for both businesses to trade from the same premises. Preliminary discussions with the landlord have indicated that he would release the business being acquired from its lease for a payment of £100,000. Combining the businesses on one site would not increase any other rent and rates figures.

- Acquiring this business could strengthen an acquirer's position in the local market by making them the market leader.

As an aside I have to comment that all this information was relatively easy for the seller and me to put together. The difficulty was going to be in trying to model the financial position of a possible acquiring business. Obviously we were looking to target a business like the one being sold. Common sense dictated that it would probably be bigger, obviously profitable, and either with cash or finance facilities available. I guess this was the clever bit – how we targeted the company that eventually bought the business.

Mark already knew who the bigger/successful players were in the market, so he could give me the names. We drew up a short list of six competitors and I got their accounts from Companies House. Eventually we chose a target business. Now, obviously, at a turnover of £4 million there was not a lot of detail at Companies House – small companies are allowed to file abbreviated accounts, which do not show things like turnover. That did not stop us from using our combined skills to model what such a business could look like in terms of profitability; the results are shown in Table 6.3.

The next stage was to ascertain how a combination of the two businesses would perform, assuming that all the profit improvement changes listed above were achieved. Assuming everything went to plan, then after three months the financial position of combined business would be as shown in Table 6.4.

As a result of combining the two businesses a new business with a turnover of £5 million with reduced costs should now be capable of producing a net profit of £1,190,000 in a full year. This is an improvement of £435,000 per annum, (£1,190,000 - £755,000).

I then applied a P/E multiple that I thought was appropriate for the printing industry, namely 6 times. Doing this, the value of the new combined business is £7,140,000, which is an improvement of £2,610,000 for the acquiring business (£435,000 × 6).

Table 6.3 Recent profit and loss statement for an acquiring business

Sales		£4,000,000
Cost of sales	60%	£2,400,000
Gross margin		£1,600,000
Overheads:		
Administration		£150,000
Management		£300,000
Directors		£200,000
Rent, rates, etc		£150,000
Depreciation		£45,000
		£845,000
Net profit		£755,000

Table 6.4 Bolting two businesses together

	Mark's		**Acquirer**		**Combined**	
Sales		£1,000,000		£4,000,000		£5,000,000
Cost of sales	60%	£600,000	60%	£2,400,000	55%	£2,750,000
Gross margin		£400,000		£1,600,000		£2,250,000
Price increase					5%	£250,000
Improved gross margin						£2,500,000
Overheads:						
Administration		£75,000		£150,000		£200,000
Management		£150,000		£300,000		£375,000
Directors		£150,000		£200,000		£275,000
Rent, rates, etc		£50,000		£150,000		£150,000
Depreciation		£15,000		£45,000		£60,000
		£440,000		£845,000		£1,060,000
Net profit		−£40,000		£755,000		£1,190,000
P/E multiple		n/a		6		6
Value of business		n/a		£4,530,000		£7,140,000

So on the face of things, by combining the two businesses a new business is created that is worth some £2,160,000 more than before. Our argument was that someone might pay up to this amount to acquire the business, less the costs involved. Table 6.5 shows these costs and the maximum price that could be justified for buying the business.

Table 6.5 Value vs the cost of acquisition

Improved business worth	£2,610,000
Less costs:	
Admin redundancies	£3,000
Management redundancies	£10,000
Directors' redundancies	£25,000
Compensation to landlord	£100,000
	£138,000
Maximum justifiable price to pay	£2,472,000

Assuming costs of some £138,000, which should be deducted from the value of the deal, the maximum justifiable purchase price is around £2,472,000.

Based on this calculation, how does a purchase price of £1 million, as wanted by the seller, sound? I think the conclusion must be that it looks to be pretty good value because of the improvement it helps make to the combined business. The message must therefore be that loss-making businesses are worth buying for an apparent premium if you can improve them and any other associated businesses. In this case we had provided a buyer with an irresistible proposition. If he bought the business for £1 million, he had a £1,472,000 margin of error even if he did not get it quite right. Mark was relaxed about payment – £500,000 up front and an 'earn out' over two years, which assured him of the rest (plus a bit more) if things turned out as planned.

Tax losses

Another sound reason for buying a business is the availability of tax losses. The business in the example we have just seen has lost £40,000 in the last year alone. It may have several years of losses, which have some value to an acquiring business that is profitable. If you buy a business that is in a similar trade to your own then its tax losses can be offset against your future profits. This is worth paying for as long as you pay less than your future tax rate. If, say, your business pays tax at an average rate of 30 per cent and a business you are buying has a tax loss of £100,000 then this is worth up to £30,000 (£100,000 @ 30 per cent) to your business. This may be another 'sweetener' for buying a loss-making business.

What about you?

Obviously I cannot suggest that you have a failing business – hopefully you have avoided that so far in your efforts to build value in your business. However, good businesses can fail due to market changes (as well as bad management). The important thing is to recognise it early and start to take remedial action – improve profitability and cash flow. If you believe that your business can do no better than it currently is under your ownership, forget your pride and ask yourself the question, 'Could someone else do a better job if they had cash and better management?' If you believe this to be the case, seriously consider selling the business to rescue/improve any value left in the business. Remember that beauty is in the eye of the beholder (buyer in your case) and they often want your business more than you do. Do not regard selling up as a failure – it is the natural conclusion for all businesses. That's what the rest of this book is about.

Chapter summary

In this chapter we have looked at how to improve and sell failing businesses. For most failing businesses you should focus on the following:

- gross margin;
- overheads;
- debtors;
- stock.

When your business is on its knees, do not try fast growth – marginal (all round) improvement is the answer. Remember the consultant's trick: put your selling price up by 5 per cent, cut cost of sales by 5 per cent, and cut overheads by 5 per cent. The result of this is twofold: vastly improved profitability (up 145 per cent in the example we saw earlier) and reduced working capital (cash to you) requirements – and that is before you start to reduce stocks and chase debtors hard.

The key message is that you need to do things differently. Unless you change the way you run the business you will continue to do the same (wrong) things. And it is made worse if you think you can grow the business out of trouble – you actually compound the damage.

7 *Grooming your business for sale*

Recognising the need to sell

I have already mentioned that businesses are not forever – many go through several owners. Selling up is a normal course of action, so do not feel guilty. The following are the many recognisable (and acceptable) reasons for wanting to sell a business; perhaps you can see your own situation here:

- Retirement/ill health – you have been in the business too long for the good of yourself or the business and need to release capital.

- Need for further investment, which you cannot or do not want to make.

- Economic or industry cycle – reaching a high point at which it makes best sense to jump.

- Merger and acquisition (M&A) activity – plenty of buyers looking for businesses to buy, so demand possibly outstrips supply.

- Changes in legislation – European and international legislation may be about to wipe out your business in a few years time or make it unprofitable for you to continue.

- Threat of competition – new or bigger competitors are making business life increasingly difficult so perhaps now is a good time to sell up.

- Growth prospects – future growth may be slowing down thereby reducing your option to add value to the business.

All of these can and do lead to a business sale. Of course the business may or may not be capable of yielding all the value needed, but we will look at how this can be addressed in this chapter. Recent experience has shown that size affects business valuation. This is reflected in the P/E (price/earnings) multiple that increases by a factor of 34 per cent for businesses that are worth over £4 million (source: *Acquisitions Monthly*). This extra value for bigger businesses is attributed to the following factors:

- more products/services;

- greater number and quality of customers;

- trading in more markets;

- usually better branding;

- frequently far higher research and development spend;

- not dependent on the owner-manager;

- not dependent on key employees.

Polishing the bonnet and tuning the engine

There is undoubtedly some similarity between selling your car and selling a business. Like a car, most businesses have a finite life – you want to unload both when they break down (go bust) or when they are looking really good (making the most money). The simple message is that while a desirable business (like a collector's car) will usually sell itself, most businesses will need optimising (grooming) for sale to get the best price (maximise its value).

Let's take the car analogy a little bit further. Those in the car trade advise me that any small dents and paint blemishes will reduce by approximately 20 per cent the value of a car being sold. Let's imagine then a used 1995

Ford Mondeo with 60,000 miles on the clock is being sold for an asking price of £2,500. If it has several dings and chips on its doors and bonnet then its value will probably drop by £500 to £2,000. The cost of remedying these is quite small – typically £50 per panel (for dents) and £50 per panel for small paintwork improvement. For this car the overall cost would be £250 but this will yield a payback of £500 – not bad, I reckon. The other benefit is that the car is more attractive and easier to sell: you therefore improve its chances of being sold.

This has dealt with the very visible aspect of selling a car, but what about under the bonnet, the steering, the brakes, etc? These are all important, but how visible are these faults to the private buyer? Probably not at all. Yes, a recent MOT certificate and service history give some comfort to the buyer, but how does he know he is not being ripped off? The usual solution is to pay a garage or a motoring organisation (like the AA or RAC) to check it out. They can subject it to a thorough inspection (100-point check) and will usually uncover any major faults. This will hopefully stop you from buying a pup, or at least give you a negotiating tool to knock the price down.

What's all this got to do with selling businesses? Well, it's pretty much the same sort of process. The way to ensure you get the best price for your business is to prepare it (groom it) for sale. You must do the equivalent of making the bodywork look good and making sure the service history is complete. You also need to sell it in the right place (we will cover that later) and be prepared for accountants and solicitors (equivalent of the AA and RAC engineers) crawling all over it. With proper grooming you will improve the value of your business by several hundred per cent. Ignore this aspect and your perfectly good business will hardly sell for net asset value. Interested? Well, read on.

Recognise the gap

Last year I helped a couple of owners sell their businesses and I am currently working with about a dozen others. I am also part of a team that delivers a programme at Cranfield University (we call it the Value Forum), which is specifically aimed at owner-managers who want to sell their businesses. The programme has a finite period, but the time it may take to get their business ready for sale and sell it is unique to each business. However, the starting point is always the same: asking the owner-manager, 'How much do you want for your business?' The usual answer is quite vague and may provoke a response like, '£10 million' – but they usually say this without too much thought. The real issue is that they have not thought about how much money they will need to continue supporting themselves, their partner and any children that have yet to finish their education for the remaining x years ahead. Most people believe that there is a fixed price for a business – a bit like the trade guides for cars. This is not the case. The starting point for valuing a business is to find out how much the seller needs. Let's say that after some reflection (and totting-up) our owner-manager comes up with £8 million as the figure that he needs to meet his future needs.

The next stage is to establish how much the business is worth today. Those of you who have looked at Chapter 4 in this book on equity funding will have a reasonable idea of the factors that influence valuation. The problem is that when you look at several factors you introduce a lot of inaccuracy. However, it is possible to value most businesses with a reasonable degree of accuracy based on the factors that I have highlighted. Let's say that as of today our owner-manager's business is worth £4 million and that he owns all of it. We can now see quite clearly (and probably to the dismay of our owner-manager) that his business is not worth what he wants.

This is what usually happens. What it tells us that there is a gap of some £3 million between the current value and the expectation of the owner-manager. I would call this 'the grooming gap', ie the extra added value that has to be applied to meet the expectation.

Ok, so we now know how much extra value we need to add (and shortly we will look at ways of doing this) but how long should this process take? Here comes the next possible disappointment. Quite frequently owner-managers will state a time, which corresponds with when they want to get out of the business, say five years. If we were to take our example again, this would mean that £4 million value needs to be added in five years, which equates to an average improvement of 20 per cent per annum (doubling of value in five years).

How much of a challenge is this? If in the last few years the value of the business has grown by only 10 per cent per annum, then this is a lot to ask. It is possible that profit improvement may not on its own yield the value required. We need therefore to examine other ways that grooming can add value over and above that yielded by purely improved profitability.

Let's look at how we can groom a business to add value – a sort of shopping list of things to do. The key things to concentrate on when grooming the business typically fall into the following five areas.

1. Financial and accounting

The obvious starting point is to examine ways of improving the company's profit performance. This will involve the following.

Margin review
To date the business will have been think long term, ie the pricing/margin strategy has probably been geared towards market penetration/seeing off the competition. The focus should now be on profit maximisation. This is the time to consider increasing prices to improve margins and thus enhance profitability during the run-up to a sale of the business.

Overhead review
Subject everything to the zero-based budgeting approach – this makes the business justify every cost. At the same time take out all excess owners' costs: salaried relatives (who do nothing in the business), excess remuneration packages, holiday homes, etc. The purpose is to show the true level of profit that the business can generate in the hands of a different owner. It is of course argued that a purchaser could add these costs back to show the true underlying profit – but it is more powerful to show that the business can run without these costs.

Balance sheet review
This is a good time to weed out all those assets that are not fully required by the business (prior to due diligence). Clear out the family yacht, the property in Provence, etc. At the same time, if assets are undervalued have them professionally valued so that you will get full value for them in the sale. Tidy up debtors (get that old money in and write of bad/dubious debtors) – treat the costs as one-offs. Do the same with stocks. Try and run a lean and mean business by making sure that working capital is reduced to a minimum. If there is excess cash in the business either take it out or make sure you get full value for this during the price negotiations. Note that the current tax regime tends to favour the latter option.

Pension schemes

If there is a company scheme that provides a pension on a final salary basis, obtain an actuarial review. If there is a surplus (often the case in older schemes) then take a full or partial pension holiday – this will give profits a boost. Of course you can remove the risk to the business altogether by converting a final salary scheme to a money purchase scheme.

Accounting system review

Good financial information inspires confidence in a buyer. Make sure you have budgets (and use them), regular monthly management accounts (including balance sheet), and a sound computerised accounting system. Also ensure that whoever is responsible for preparing the accounts is technically competent – look to recruit a qualified accountant if you are lacking.

Accounting policy review

When you are selling a business it is vital that profit is maximised, which means making sure that you take profit at the right time. Look at your contract accounting to make sure you take profit as soon as is possible. Check out your depreciation and amortisation policies to see if they can be made less aggressive to claw back profit.

2. Operational

If I have not said it already, then I must say it now: a business is nothing without good management and staff. Far too often a business is too dependent on the owner-manager for leadership, management and technical expertise. A large part of your grooming process must be to demonstrate that your business has moved away from this situation. You should show the proof of the following.

Devolved management control

Demonstrate that second-line managers are making executive decisions by tangible records of this, such as minutes of management meetings, proper job descriptions/titles, and a formal organisation chart with reporting lines identified.

Board strength

Make sure that all major disciplines are represented at board level, eg finance, sales and marketing, operations, human resources, as well as a managing director. This helps show that the business is not run by one person – strategy can be devised and carried out by the board. Appoint recognised non-executive directors to supplement areas where the board is weak.

Incentive schemes

Any buyer will want to be sure that the management team will stay on and be well motivated under the new owners. Bonus schemes and share options related to company performance are a good way of achieving this. Linked to good service contracts this should inspire confidence in a buyer that the important staff will stay.

Staff reviews

Make sure that all pay reviews, appraisals and redundancies have been completed prior to the start of negotiations. Get the staff cost right for the proposed level of business. If you make any redundancies, do so well in advance of the sale negotiations, otherwise this may be treated as unfair dismissal by an industrial tribunal.

3. Legal and administration

I bet you had not thought this was an area for grooming a business to improve value – wrong. It is all part of the process of tidying up your house to prevent problems at the due diligence stage (we will look at this later). Carry out a legal audit – use your solicitor to help you. The key things to look at are the following.

Outstanding litigation

Buyers hate uncertainty and will fear the worst of any situation. If, for example, you have an ex-employee taking you to an industrial tribunal, resolve this as part of your grooming activity. In all probability the real cost may be, for example, £10,000. In the eyes of a buyer this could escalate to £50,000. At a P/E ratio of 10 this could make as much as a £400,000 (£40,000 x 10) reduction in the value of your business. The clear message must be:

get it sorted so that it becomes a known liability as opposed to an uncertain liability. In all probability even this £10,000 can be shown to be a one-off cost that will be excluded from the valuation.

Employment contracts with key staff

Obviously all employees must have employment contracts once they have been with the business for the statutory period. This shows the outside world (including buyers) that you do things properly. It also reduces the future potential for legal action by disgruntled employees if the rules are in place. Those employees who are key to the success of the sale (and are not shareholders) need to be rewarded in some way to ensure that they are a positive force in making the sale successful. This can take the form of a rolling 12-month employment contract, which ensures that if the new owners don't want them they will get at least 12 months' salary (usually tax-free). It can also take the form of a cash bonus when the business is sold (for the target price).

Title deeds and leases

You are going to need these when you sell the business, so find them now. At the same time make sure that they say what you think they do. For example, if you lease your premises and they are important to the successful sale of the business, then do make sure that the business has the benefit of continued use of them when it is sold. My thoughts are that if it will take two years to groom the business for sale and you have only one year left on the lease, you have uncertainty. Talk to your landlord now to find out if the lease can be renewed at the end of this period – and on what terms. Get agreement in writing now for, say, a further three years. You may find that this will delight your landlord and that he may forgo any rent increase. This gives your new buyer security of tenure for at least two years, which is probably long enough. Do not tie the new owner in much longer than this – they may want to relocate the business to improve the value to them. This will be reflected in the price they want to offer.

Intellectual property

If your business has patents, trademarks, etc, then make sure they are registered. This gives them full value. Also make sure that they are in the company's name. You do not want to find part-way through the sale that these are not registered or that they do not belong to the company. This creates uncertainty and will affect the price – it may be the final straw that forces a buyer to walk away from the deal.

Trading contracts

It may seem obvious, but if your business is dependent on key customers and/or suppliers you should be reducing the risk. Putting in place supplier contracts for key supplies will help ensure that you can continue to trade in difficult times – world shortages, rising prices, indifferent quality, etc. On the other side of the coin it makes a buyer (of your business) feel really good if they can see that a large percentage of your future sales are already guaranteed by reference to trading contracts. Make sure that if you sell the business all these contracts can be passed over to the new owner without any restrictions – this may mean rewriting some of the wording.

Complicated company structures

If for some historic reason your business has several trading companies with different shareholders, this will become a nightmare when the legal stage of the sale starts. A buyer wants simplicity. This may mean buying out minority shareholders and restructuring the business as just one company or as a true group, ie a parent company with 100 per cent ownership of its subsidiaries.

Shareholder agreements

Older companies may not have articles of association and memoranda that provide for how to deal with the sale of the business. It is common to have shareholder agreements that state in writing how shares can be bought and sold, either as part of a complete business sale or by an individual shareholder wishing to get out of the business. Get your solicitor to run their eye over your articles/memorandum and shareholder agreements to make sure they are ok.

Accounts filing, board minutes, tax

Do make sure that everything is up to date and that there are no outstanding tax bills (corporation tax/National Insurance/PAYE) or that the company is about to be struck off for late filing of accounts.

4. Vendor due diligence

Due diligence is the process by which the buyer tries to ensure that what they are buying is what they see – it's a bit like getting the AA or RAC to check out the car you are buying. In its simplest form it involves a person (usually an accountant) working from a pre-prepared comprehensive checklist to make sure everything is in apple pie order. It will flush out many of the things that we have looked at earlier in this chapter. If anything is not in order it will be identified and used by the buyer to negotiate the price downwards.

Of course the smart thing to do is to stop this from ever happening. This can be done by the seller (vendor) arranging for due diligence to be carried out. This is similar to the idea that the UK government tried to pilot recently in the housing market by way of a seller's pack that contained title deeds, searches, survey, etc. The idea was to speed things up and make sure that no nasties appeared during the process. By carrying out vendor due diligence you have the opportunity to see what nasties the accountant has spotted in your business and do something about it before the buyer spots it.

Vendor due diligence involves the seller instructing accountants to prepare a due diligence report. The key things to note are that a) you must use independent accountants (not your auditors) from a national firm (the top six), which inspires confidence for the buyer; and b) the report belongs to the buyer – this report is paid for by the seller but they do not tell the accountant what to do. The accountants' report is made available to the favoured buyer.

5. Other

There are a few other things that you can do to groom your business for sale that do not comfortably fall within the previous headings. They are all designed to show a prospective buyer that this is a tidy and well-ordered business.

Business plan and strategy
If you do not have a business plan then you have arrived at this point by luck together with some good judgement. A prospective purchaser will view

a business plan as a real strength. It can be used to show that your growth budgets have some sound logic and substance to them. It can be used to demonstrate your knowledge of the market, competitors, etc. Its purpose is to show that the business has a sound strategy for growth.

Environmental audit
If you own your premises you are responsible for any pollution they cause in addition to any effluent that your type of trade may cause. This will be of concern to a buyer who may be uncertain of how much it may cost them to put it right. The answer is to get an independent specialist to carry out an environmental audit to quantify any problem and get it sorted. Your business will then have a clean bill of health.

Smarten up the premises
During the business selling process you will have numerous visitors (which you must control) who will be influenced by first impressions. Don't spend a fortune, but smarten up both the outside and inside of your offices/works.

Public relations/brand awareness
A business is worth far more if it has a name and products/services that are known. The objective is to raise the profile of the business, not just in the eyes of customers, but also in the eyes of buyers. Target the financial and trade press. Also, you can use PR to create a smoke screen during the sale process. You could leak a story that the company is considering a public flotation – this will help explain the increase in 'suits' appearing at your company.

The overall objective is to create an appearance of a well-ordered, optimised business that needs nothing doing to it to continue to turn out good and improving levels of profit. Listen to what Chris Hutt has to say on grooming businesses for sale.

Case study: Chris Hutt

Chris Hutt has established an enviable reputation as a developer of pub retailing businesses. To date he has started several and sold on others. In all he has made some £11 million capital profit in doing what he enjoys. The *Financial Times* said of one of his deals, 'Mind blowing. Breaking all valuation records.' When talking to a group of owner-managers he had the following key messages on grooming for sale to maximise the value of a business:

- Brand. Never underestimate the value of a brand. Richard Branson has created and extended this to new heights – some people may think he has gone too far. Chris has created numerous brands, such as the 'Newt and Cucumber', 'Wizard Inns', 'Unicorns Inns', and 'Midsummer Inns'. The important thing was that these created a value that was long lasting and over and above the underlying profit-based value of the business. His brands created envy in the eyes of his competitors.

- Image. Chris never missed an opportunity to tell the world about how well his business was doing. He used PR to make sure that the trade (his competitors and possible buyers of his business) was always reading about his business and the success it was having. The image that he created was bigger than the business itself.

- Growth curve. I can subscribe to this one because we used it when we floated our company on AIM in 1998. The trick, says Chris, is to create a steep growth curve (sales and profit) over several years – this hooks buyers. However, as a postscript to this, do make sure that you show that this growth will continue for at least another 18 months, just to show that there is something left from which a buyer can reap the benefit.

- Multiple expansion. All markets and industries go through cycles in terms of confidence and profitability. The trick is to time your growth curve (see above) to your industry cycle. If you can make these two coincide, this will enhance the P/E that is achieved. Always aim to sell when both are on the upward curve – not at the peak.

- Auction. Not strictly part of the grooming process, but certainly a great way to improve value. When you are going through the grooming process try and identify several buyers and shortlist a handful. Through your brand and image activities make sure these people are aware that your business may be available. Chris says that he got some six parties interested when he was selling one of his businesses. This brought two formal offers, which he set off against each other as an auction. The initial offer of £7 million eventually became a firm offer of £12 million.

Some serious words of wisdom from someone who is a serial business seller. Chris also had a few other words of wisdom on grooming and creating value:

- People. They are key to any business. If they are well motivated they will perform miracles to help grow your business. Chris stressed that you should always have a personal touch with your staff – this lets them know you care. Take time to write cards if it's their birthday or some other important event has happened. He is a great believer in sending them small gifts if they have performed 'above and beyond' the call of duty.

- Advisers. Always use people you know or are recommended by people you trust. Obviously for Chris, a serial seller of businesses, this made sense since he was likely to work with them again. The other gem he discovered is that if you are choosing advisers for the first time, have a 'beauty parade'. Obviously choose those you feel there is a chemistry and understanding with and pay them by results, ie let them share in the risk with you.

- Board of directors/shareholders. Make sure that you can control your board of directors. In Chris's words, 'Make sure you are all singing off the same hymn sheet and make sure there are no chinks in your armour.' I would add shareholders. There can be nothing worse, when trying to sell a business, than to have a minority shareholder trying to queer the whole deal or driving down the price. Agree the deal with all shareholders before trying to sell the business.

Chris was totally committed to the important task of grooming a business for sale and what he did looks like real common sense. However, there are some things that you may never think of doing that can improve the business.

Case study: Jim Smith

In 2001 my friend Jim Smith sold his business for £8 million in cash. There was no doubt that it was a nice business, but the average sales growth and profitability over the last couple of years were not exceptional. In the most recent year's accounts (12 months to 31 December 2000) the sales were just £3 million with operating profits of £400,000. Our concern was that this was late June 2001 and these figures were looking a little old to us, and we wondered what our buyers might think of figures that were nearly six months out of date. Ideally we wanted to show some figures to 30 June. These would be bang up to date and also correspond with the year-end of the company we were targeting as a buyer. The decision was taken to restate the figures on this basis for the last two years up to 30 June 2001. Obviously the figures for June 2001 would be an estimate, but we had sufficient data (sales, costs, etc) to give pretty good figures for this month. Also remember that June would be just one-twelfth of the year to 30 June 2001 figures, so 11 months (the bulk) were actual figures.

So what was the end result of our restating of the figures? Very interesting. The year to 30 June 2001 showed turnover of £4 million and operating profit of £550,000. The comparable figures for the year to 30 June 2000 showed turnover of £2.5 million and operating profit of £300,000. Quite suddenly it made the business appear to have had dramatic sales growth (60 per cent) and profit growth (83 per cent). This was enough to make the prospect's eyes water. This also enabled the business to project 'cautious' growth figures for the following year that were incredibly attractive. The business was sold within three months.

It's all about timing

Many of the actions listed above are common sense – I am sure that most people will see the value in doing these things to groom their businesses. However, a question of timescale must now come into play. How long does it typically take to groom a business for sale? Well, I'm afraid there is not a definitive answer to this. My experience is that where a business needs only cosmetic improvement – tidying up as I call it – then this can typically be done within 12 months. If, however, more radical surgery is required, such as profit improvement, then I would say two years would be nearer the mark.

The most common situation is where owner-managers reach a point in their life where they decide that they want to sell up. After some discussion with their adviser they determine how much cash they will need to fund their future life. I must make a brief comment on this process. Unless you are a serial entrepreneur you usually only have one chance to sell a business – so do not sell yourself short. Make sure that you have calculated an adequate capital sum to meet your future needs. Age, family circumstances and lifestyle will all have a part to play in determining the capital value that the sale of your business needs to provide for you. This then is the target value that the grooming process must aim to achieve. The reality is usually that this is a value some two to three times greater than the current valuation of the business – a daunting task you may think. Yes. In fact, just as I am writing this book I have a live example of how this whole process is panning out for one of my clients – a husband and wife team who own a small marketing communications business in Coventry.

Case study: Tim and Linda Holmes

Tim and Linda Holmes started their business some years ago, shortly after Tim graduated from art college. Over the years the business has had good times and bad. I can remember just a couple of years ago when Tim, Linda (his wife and co-director) and I sat in a room to make a survival plan. However, the business has moved on and as we stand now it employs 32 people and this year it should turn over about £2.1 million and make pre-tax profits in the region of £300,000. I have crudely valued the business at between £1 million and £1.5 million. I will not bore you with all the details of how I did this but it did take into account all the usual factors – industry, size of business, management team, historic performance, etc. After some discussion with Tim and Linda they told me what their lifestyle ambitions were. Based on these (and the fact that Tim is only just 40) they reckoned they needed £3 million to fund this.

So the task then is simple – double the value of the business. Tim had indicated to me that they wanted out, or at least the option to get out within four years. So that set the maximum timescale. However, my suggestion was that we could achieve it within the next three financial years. What we did was model how the business could be grown to achieve this valuation. Key to this was empowering the management team to take over the operational decision-making. Next will be promoting the most able to director status. Within two years Tim should have a business that can run without his day-to-day involvement.

Together we reviewed all the clients and devised a strategy to grow and service each. Quite honestly the business, if it continues its current growth, will easily turn over £3 million and make a profit of around £500,000. Together with the other 'quality' improvements, this business will comfortably be worth his target figure. I have told them that I want to get them in excess of £5 million when we sell it.

What about your business grooming?

This is the time for the ultimate honesty about your business – just how good is it? You will probably need help with coming up with the answer. If you have a trusted adviser, get them to rate your business and give you a crude valuation. Now you know the truth. The next moment of truth is about timing. How much longer before you want out? If the timescale is less than two years then I think you may have a problem. Two years may not give you enough time to groom your business to extract maximum value, unless it is already peaking in terms of profit performance. Assuming that you can hang on for a longer period, then devise your grooming plan following the guidance in this chapter.

The final word of advice is to try and sell your business without selling it – yes, I know it sounds odd. The trick is to get a steady queue of people asking whether your business might be for sale. How do you do that? Well, we cover that and some more on the selling process in the next chapter.

Chapter summary

In this chapter we have looked at the process of improving businesses to enhance their value prior to sale. We call this 'grooming', and it can take anywhere between one and three years, depending on the scale of the improvement needed. The aspects of grooming are quite simple:

- Step 1 – improve the real or apparent profitability.

- Step 2 – get it running smoothly without the need for the involvement of the owner-manager.

- Step 3 – tidy up the administration by making sure all the contracts are in place: employment, suppliers, customers, intellectual property, premises, etc.

- Step 4 – Make sure you can present the buyer with a business neatly wrapped up for sale, ie due diligence done and in apple pie order.

As a final word of advice – make sure you start the process early. It's never too early to start the process of grooming your business. Do not leave it until it's too late – you will never get the best price for a business if you are rushed into a sale. If you have decided you want to retire/ sell up in five years' time then start the grooming process now. Grooming will be a gentle process. If you want to get out in two years' time then you had better get your skates on. Unless the business is already ready for sale your grooming process is going to become more hurried and aggressive.

8

Exit routes

Are you ready to sell?

By now your business is hopefully at peak value – the result of all your hard grooming effort. I know that this may seem like a silly question but I do need to ask it at this stage, especially before you start to take on advisers, accountants, solicitors, lawyers, etc and the costs start to pile up. Are you ready to sell your business – emotionally? Believe me, strange things happen to owner-managers when it comes time to consider letting go of their businesses. Suddenly that business that they started 15 years ago, invested so much of their life in (maybe even sacrificed a marriage over), grown up with and got used to, and which is now a lovely business (as a result of all that grooming) has become just too impossible to let go of. The emptiness – what will they do with their time now they have nothing to do? Ok, so you think I'm laying it on a bit thick, but let me give three real case studies to ponder on.

Colin Barrow

Colin Barrow (yes, my dad) left the Army when he was about 55. He had a full Army pension – that was the deal they were offering for what they called 'compulsory retirement'. He had, by careful investment, made a small fortune on the stock market during the 1960s and 1970s – well, without a war going on he did have a lot of time on his hands. Both he and my mother had financial security ahead of them, not a worry in the world. Within a month he was bored out of his mind. The transition from organised life (you could say regimented) to retirement at a comparatively young age was unbearable. Within three months he was working again – restoring pictures, reframing, etc in a small gallery near where they lived in Harrogate. Within 10 years he was dead, having never really got used to 'civvy life'. Just three more years on and my mother was dead – sort of gave up after my dad had died.

The moral of this story: you need to be ready for significant life changes – it needs years of planning. It needs the full involvement of all the family.

George Ryman

George Ryman and his two brothers run a very successful business. They could sell the business any day for £25 million plus – split three ways that would still do very nicely. One of the issues is that the three brothers are all of different ages, ranging from mid-40s to mid-60s. One of the brothers, recovering from heart trouble, needs to ease off a bit. The oldest brother really ought to be thinking about cutting back and planning for retirement. The youngest brother, George, is not sure that he wants to give up working. If they were to sell he may want to start up another business. So they all have different needs, not necessarily resolved by having a bucketful of cash. I have spoken to them all and I feel that making a decision to sell will be very difficult. Also, I get the impression that while we have talked about selling there is a tremendous feeling of guilt around the boardroom. They think they will be letting down the workforce if they 'sell out' (their words, not mine). One of them is haunted by the feeling that they would be selling the family silver, and concerned about whether they will have got the best price.

The moral of this story: this is a family decision – three brothers, three wives, several children, and some grandparents are involved. It almost needs a family conference to agree the decision to sell: only then will it feel right for the three brothers.

Allan Rimmer

Allan Rimmer owns (with his wife) a temporary recruitment agency called Network Midlands. I have known him for nearly 10 years but our paths have only crossed again recently. With some 12 branches he had thought about grooming his business for sale. He was bringing on board a management team, but there were still some organisational issues to resolve. Things were, however, pretty well sorted and he and his wife enjoyed a really good lifestyle, jetting off to international conferences. We sat down and started to plot how the grooming process could go. The focus was very much on a sale.

One day we were talking about the business and Allan quizzed me about shares and directorships. Obviously he was thinking about how he could keep his key managers without giving away equity. For many years Allan and his wife had traded as a partnership – the change to limited company status had been quite recent. We devised a structure that enabled him to have a series of regional/area boards beneath a main board. His managers could progress from office manager to being a member of an area board. The best of these could then become regional managing director and eventually rise to the full board. All this could be done without sacrificing any equity. The use of imaginative titles containing the word 'director', a better car and an improved remuneration package would offer the carrot needed. A month later I met Allan and he had made two profound decisions. He was not selling up (not for the foreseeable future anyway) and his wife had decided to exit the business in six months' time.

The moral of this story: Allan had seen a way to keep the baby that he really loved (his business) and was an important part of his life – he needed it, but his wife did not. She could get out and was going to.

These three examples are not exceptional. They reveal a little of the complexity of people leaving behind something that has been an important part of their life. My observation is that there must be some planning to cope with the emotional side of selling a business. Here are some thoughts that may help.

You need a plan for the rest of your life

Just as you needed a business plan, you have to give serious consideration to what you are going to do with the rest of your life. Remember, if you are selling up at, say, 40 then you could easily have another 30 to 40 years ahead of you. This is a long time for your money to last (if you are planning not to work again) and a long time to amuse yourself. People who have been single-minded in their business life (ie sacrificed family life and hobbies, leisure, etc) have a real problem. Start your hobbies before you sell up.

Involve your family – all businesses are 'family' businesses. There are the needs of others to consider. If you are planning to become a tax exile in Belgium (some people have done this) then find out what your spouse or partner and teenage children think – I suspect they will say, 'You go, we'll stay here.' Make sure everybody is happy with the arrangements.

Don't feel guilty

If you have sold your business and are leaving your employees behind, remember that you have run all the risks (like the early days of personal guarantees, etc) and given them continued employment for many years. You will have done your best to protect them in terms of continued employment by selling to a company that wants to maintain the business. You can do no more – you are not their parent.

Did I get the best price possible?

Do not torment yourself with this question. The best way to avoid this is by not accepting the first offer you get – get a better offer. If you have been helped by a half-way decent adviser they will make sure you get the best deal. Remember what I wrote in the chapter on value: 'How do I know if I have got the best price for my business? When you would not buy back your own business for the amount you have just sold it for.' If you get an offer that meets your personal requirements then take it and shut the book on the past. If you cannot achieve this, then either do not sell your business or sell 90 per cent to get most of the cash that you want and retain 10 per cent to sell at some future date.

The options

There are really only three acceptable ways of selling a business to realise maximum value. These are:

1. Trade sale – you sell out to another company, usually a larger competitor, or a supplier, or a 'shot from the blue' by some little known business choosing to diversify. Trade sales are normally used to sell 100 per cent of the equity.
2. Private equity – a financial institution buys your business. This may be done to provide the cash for a management buy-out (MBO), management buy-in (MBI) or buy-in management buy-out (BIMBO). Private equity can be used for full or partial sell out of equity.
3. Public market – the business is 'floated' on the stock market. This is usually by means of an Alternative Investment Market (AIM) listing or a full or main Stock Exchange listing. The public market is almost always used for a partial sale of equity.

Each has its own characteristics and not all are appropriate for all businesses. Let's examine each in a little more detail.

1. Trade sale

This is the most likely disposal route for most companies – to be sold to another company. Quite frequently the acquiring business is a quoted company, because for them buying privately owned businesses is comparatively cheap. Why should this be, I hear you ask. It's all to do with the inherent advantage that a company with access to money and a free market in its shares (ie, a company listed on the Stock Exchange) has over a privately owned company that has no free movement in its shares. Let me give you an example.

Case study

A medium-sized quoted media company (turnover c £100 million) is looking to acquire a smaller privately owned business in the same market place. A quick review of the *Financial Times* reveals that this company has a P/E of 15. This is slightly above average for the sector but reflects the performance of this business and the esteem that it is held in by the financial institutions. Its shares are frequently bought and sold on the Stock Exchange and in recent months its share price has been on the rise. Contrast this with the smaller privately owned business (turnover c £5 million) in which the family shares have never been freely bought and sold. It has performed well and as a result of the grooming process is being sold at a P/E of 7. This is not an uncommon situation for a typical trade sale.

Let's add some more specific numbers to see how the deal could work; see Table 8.1.

The quoted company made profits of £4 million last year and based on its high P/E of 15 has a market capitalisation (value) of £60 million (£4 million × 15). Compare this with the private company, which made profits of £500k but because of its lower P/E of 7 is

Table 8.1 Quoted vs unquoted company

	Quoted company (before)	**Private company**	**Quoted company (after)**
Profit	£4,000,000	£500,000	£4,500,000
P/E	15	7	15
Value	£60,000,000	£3,500,000	£67,500,000

valued at just £3.5 million. If the quoted company were to acquire this business its value would improve to £67.5 million. This is done simply by bolting the acquired profit stream onto its own (assuming that profit levels would be maintained) and using the quoted company's P/E ratio. The stock market would not differentiate between acquired and generated profits in the hands of the acquiring quoted company.

So what does this mean? Quite simply the quoted company can afford to pay £7.5 million (£67.5m - £60m) for a company worth £3.5 million. In other words it can afford to pay well over the odds to buy a smaller privately owned businesses. A similar advantage applies to larger unquoted private companies – but not to such an extent. This is why trade sales are the number one route for owner-managers wanting to sell up.

Inexpensive and fast

The other good news about trade sales is they are comparatively cheap to achieve (no stockbrokers, nominated advisers, financial PR, etc). You are dealing with people who understand your type of business/industry, so there is no need for expensive lawyers and top-notch accountants. You can stick with your current auditors (because to be honest they may have minimal involvement in the process). Most competent lawyers can handle the legal side, and in fact most of it is driven by the trade buyer, who will write the contracts. The biggest cost could be the 2 to 3 per cent that you might have to pay an intermediary to find a buyer, unless you can do it yourself. A final cost will be that involved in preparing the selling package to get your company sold. Fortunately, if you read the next chapter you can further reduce these costs.

Where the other exit routes typically take four to six months to achieve – a public market float could take a year or more to plan and execute – a trade sale could be completed in three months. Just recently my friends Jim and Steve (we will see more about them in the next chapter) sold their business. We prepared the selling package in late June 2001 and the cheque cleared in early September 2001. In the meantime the buyer completed due diligence and everything else it needed to make sure it was happy with what it was buying. Fast – you can barely buy a house quicker than that these days.

Higher prices

Because trade buyers have at least one other business to bolt yours onto they can get business improvement from acquiring your business. In other words 1 + 1 = 3 or synergy, as it is often called. This can mean that marginal businesses (remember Chapter 6 on debt-bound and failing businesses) frequently sell for good prices – you would never get this kind of deal from a public market flotation. You probably would not get a MBO deal for this kind of business either.

2. Private equity

A management buy-out (MBO) is where outside funding is used to support the existing management team in buying out the business. Typically the management will establish a small share holding together with a venture capitalist (private equity) buying the bulk of the shares. There are two mechanisms for buying a company. The favoured route (for venture capitalists) is to set up a new limited company (referred to as 'NewCo'). This then buys those parts of the balance sheet that it wants (at an agreed price) together with ongoing business (customers, services/products, suppliers, staff, etc) for which it also pays an agreed price. The advantage of this process is that a clean purchase is made and the risk of any nasties such as tax liabilities, redundancy/wrongful dismissal actions, claims form customers/suppliers crawling out of the woodwork later are reduced.

Alternatively, the shares of the company can be bought outright by the management team and venture capitalist. In this situation the company remains intact and ownership (together with all the inherent liabilities as well as assets) just passes over to new faces. In terms of cost (legal and accounting) a straight purchase of shares is the cheaper option.

When does it occur?
Buy-outs may be seller motivated or buyer motivated.

Seller-motivated buy-outs arise due to:

- succession problems: family-owned companies, where the owners want to avoid the publicity of a trade sale;

- lack of strategic fit: a parent company wanting to sell a subsidiary that does not fit into its mainstream business;

- sale of a subsidiary that is encountering significant financial problems and poor performance;

- sale to raise urgently needed cash for other acquisitions or survival.

Buyer motivated buy-outs may be inspired by the urge to be free from the bureaucracy of corporate control and the entrepreneurial urge to make money for themselves.

What makes MBOs so popular?

- *For managers:* other than starting their own business, an MBO provides the best opportunity for managers to be their own boss and to be financially successful. They know the business well, the risks are lower and the probability of success is higher.

- *For the existing owners:* a buy-out provides a method for releasing capital tied up in the business, an opportunity to reward the existing management team for past services, and a way of preserving the independence and continuity of the company.

- *For the investors:* a buy-out is an opportunity to invest in a business with a strong track record and a dedicated management team. In effect it becomes a lower risk investment.

How to carry out your MBO

1.*The management team.* Don't make the team too big – five is a sensible number. Has each individual the ability to run their own business alongside a financial backer (who may or may not interfere)? Is each individual committed for the long term to the success of the venture? Allocate responsibilities – make sure finance, sales/marketing, operations, admin and legal are all covered. Good communications between the team are essential, but it is impossible for all decisions to be taken by committee. The leader must have a proven track record of success and their team must be able to prove their professional competency.

2. *Professional advisers.* You will need lawyers and accountants. Areas where you will require advice from lawyers include: company setting up/ changing articles of association, memorandum, etc; contracts; employment; intellectual property; property; and security (for the banking facilities).

Areas where you will require advice from accountants include: accounting and reporting systems and controls; assistance with the business plan (the plan must be drafted by the management team, but the figures must be validated by a respected firm of accountants); price; and raising and structuring finance.

It is essential that the lawyers and accountants work as a team supporting the management. There are areas where the lawyers' and the accountants' roles overlap and this ought to be clarified at an early stage. Areas of possible overlap include: acting as a sounding board for the business plan (you should probably allow overlap on this); tax warranties, indemnities and clearances; employee share schemes and pension arrangements; and finance documents.

Points to note on professional fees include: NewCo will usually pay the professional fees. The management team may be able to negotiate that the balance of the fees is payable on a contingent basis (ie contingent on completion of the transaction). This will depend on the transaction. The team might have to pay fees if the MBO fails. On successful completion the fees will be funded by the equity investors through their investment in NewCo.

3. *Sellers.* Employees (and that includes the MBO team) owe a fiduciary duty to their employers. They must act honestly and the interests of their employer must remain paramount. Thus in any MBO there are conflicts between duties to the employer and personal interests. To deal with these potential conflicts, the sellers will usually set guidelines (particularly with regard to the supply of information), which must be followed. The sellers will seek a level playing field between the MBO team and other buyers – although the MBO team will usually be the favoured buyer. Remember that the sellers too are balancing competing objectives. Their concerns will include: their need to be able to demonstrate that they have negotiated the highest price reasonably obtainable for the business, especially if a publicly quoted company; they will want to ensure that service and other standards are maintained during the sale process and that, if applicable, there is no breach of the European Union public procurement directives or compulsory competitive tendering legislation.

Remember also that if the buy-out fails, the business might either be closed down or sold to another purchaser. Any prospective purchaser, however, may feel that anyone involved in a failed management buy-out will not be committed to the new employer. Alternatively, the new purchaser may criticise senior managers who have failed to pursue a management buy-out bid as lacking sufficient initiative, creativity or self-motivation. It depends on the culture of the successful purchaser.

4. *Business plan.* The business plan is key. It is essential for the management team as a group to thrash out the draft business plan. It is a mistake to have it drafted initially by the professional advisers, as it is the team who must have ownership of it and be committed to delivering what it promises. The British Venture Capital Association produces a booklet on business plans and financing proposals. This provides a useful guide as to what investors will be looking for, and a copy will be provided on request (see Sources of help at the back of this book).

5. *Price.* At an early stage in the process you ought to review the net asset value of the business and also make preliminary calculations on the price so that you can start thinking about likely source of funding. While the maximum price will depend on cash flow projections and an assessment of future maintainable profits together with net assets acquired, the actual price depends on whether a competitive bidder emerges. While you must act honestly you do not wish to provoke competition for the business. Remember at all times that buyers only want to pay the minimum price that will secure them the business.

6. *Private equity investors.* The key is to try and have them compete against each other for the business. Generally, though, the final terms offered by each are very similar. Ultimately the choice will be yours based on how well you feel you relate to the organisation offering you money. The venture capitalist will want to see financial commitment from each senior member of the management team. In a normal commercial venture you would expect each manager to invest between six months' and one year's salary in the new business. This may not always be practical, but no investor is going to put in their money to back management unless they are satisfied that the management is committed to making it a success. The investor will want to know that you will hang on by your fingernails if necessary to ensure the business succeeds.

7. *Finance.* An MBO is likely to include one or more of the following:

- ordinary shares subscribed for by the management;
- preference shares subscribed for by the venture capitalists (these will be the same as ordinary shares but have minority protection rights and also preferred dividend rights);

- redeemable preference shares (now known as 'institutional loan notes'), which give rights to a fixed dividend, generally have very limited voting rights and rank behind the ordinary creditors of the company, but have priority over the ordinary shareholders;

- term loan secured by fixed and floating charges on all the assets of the company, also known as 'senior debt', typically over five to seven years;

- mezzanine debt, which is unsecured debt with a higher rate of interest and with some equity involvement but not repayable until after the senior debt;

- bank overdraft.

Larger MBOs can include various other forms of financial instruments (eg a loan with options to subscribe for shares).

A typical deal is funded as a mixture of all the above, usually in the ratio of 60 per cent debt from the bank (term loans) and 40 per cent by the private equity house and management team. Usually the management team will only provide around 1 per cent of the total funding and the private equity house will provide most of their funding as loan stock – debt, in other words. In fact the private equity house will provide as little as 3 per cent of the total funding as equity. This would be an example of a leveraged buy-out (LBO). One of the purposes of using a large proportion of debt is to enable the management team to have a significant minority stake in return for their limited funding ability. In the above example they would acquire 25 per cent of the ordinary shares for their 1 per cent equity stake – the balance of 75 per cent would be held by the private equity house. Table 8.2 shows this.

In addition, an equity ratchet will be in place to enable the management to improve their minority shareholding if they can significantly improve the company's profitability.

8. *Legal documents.* These will include:

- Offer from the equity investor. Initially you should concentrate on the amount, rate and percentage of equity. The offer will contain: amount of investment; security, interest and terms of repayment (if appropriate); control over future transactions (such as further

Table 8.2 Typical MBO funding

Sources of funds (at completion)		Share of equity %	Share of funding %
Management – ordinary shares	163	20	1
Private equity – ordinary shares	653	75	3
Private equity – institutional loan notes	11,184		56
Total equity	12,000		
Senior debt (5 to 7 years)	6,000		30
Mezzanine debt	2,000	5	10
Total debt	8,000		
Total funding to acquire business (Ongoing)	20,000	100	100
Bank overdraft	2,000		
	22,000		

borrowings); warranties to be given by the management as to the present status of the business; fees and expenses; share rights (eg dividend and voting rights). An investor will state conditions, which must be satisfied prior to injecting funds. These are known as 'conditions precedent'.

- Agreement to purchase the business. The detail of this depends on whether you are buying an existing entity or are buying the actual individual assets and goodwill.

- Articles of Association. These set out the manner in which the company is to be governed and deals with matters such as powers of directors; rights of different classes of shareholders; procedure relating to the allotment and transfer of shares.

- Employment contracts. Investors in the company will wish to have some control over employment contracts. On the one hand they will wish the managers to be well motivated to succeed, but on the other hand they will prefer the managers to receive a reasonable remuneration and seek real wealth generation through the increase in value of their shares.

9. *Timing.* Obviously how long it will take to complete the MBO will vary according to the circumstances. For example, a friend of mine bought a subsidiary of a public company using private equity and from start to finish the deal took nearly a year. He finished up exhausted from the endless meetings, but he and his management team got the company they wanted (at not a bad price, I must add). However, a privately owned business being sold as a retirement disposal to the management team could take only three months. On average most MBOs take around six months.

10. *Specific problem areas:*

- The Transfer of Undertakings (Protection of Employment) Regulations 1981 ('TUPE') will most probably apply to all business sales, whether shares or assets. They carry significant consequences for the purchaser. The contracts of employment of existing employees automatically transfer to the purchaser on the same terms and conditions (except for certain rights under occupational pension schemes). The effects of TUPE cannot be excluded by agreement. A dismissal connected with a TUPE transfer is automatically unfair unless it is for an 'economic, technical or organisational reason entailing changes in the workforce'. Beware!

The management buy-out team should ask the seller to warrant workforce information. This encourages full and accurate disclosure as the management team may have a claim if problems occur after completion.

- Pensions. These are an important aspect of any buy-out. Consideration should be given to what (if any) pension arrangements are to be offered to employees having existing pension entitlements. It may be possible to take over the running of the pension scheme to which the employees belong. More commonly, a new pension scheme will be established with a transfer payment being negotiated from the seller's scheme to the new scheme. TUPE does not currently require a purchaser to provide pension benefits of the same type and level as those provided by the seller. A number of current court cases are challenging this and so the position may change.

- While the management buy-out team are currently free (in most cases) to take decisions on a commercial basis, it is advisable that they provide a comparable package pending the outcome of these cases. They can always agree specific terms with individual employees. It should also be noted that factors such as the average age of the workforce and the strength of any trade unions might be relevant. In practice, as much as possible of the detail of the benefits to be provided by any new scheme should be decided in advance of the buy-out. In most cases, an actuary should be instructed to assist with this.

- Intellectual property. A review of the intellectual property rights of the business would constitute part of the due diligence exercise. In relation to patents (granted and applied for), registered designs, unregistered design rights, copyright in industrial drawings and in computer software, brands and service marks and trade secrets, the following should be established: rights owned outright; rights licensed from others; rights licensed to others; other third-party rights restricting the company's ability to use them. Advice will also be necessary as to future requirements of the intellectual property.

- Employee involvement. If employees are to be involved, consideration will need to be given to the form of such involvement. For example, this can be either through an 'Esop' (Employee Share Ownership Plan) trust or through a saving scheme. In buy outs from local authorities and government, for instance, the involvement of employees in ownership is regarded as politically desirable. It provides an element of protection for the employees as a whole where interests might otherwise be seen as prejudiced in order to increase the wealth of the new owner-managers. It also produces a feel-good factor among the workforce. However, it potentially creates a number of problems. If the employees, as a body, hold a significant minority of the shares, then their agreement to any future sale or purchase needs to be obtained.

A few final words of caution on MBOs

You will notice that the bulk of the funding is in the form of debt; quite commonly up to 70 per cent of the funding comes this way. Common sense tells us (hopefully) that in growth markets with plenty of profit to be made, this can work – remember the golden years under Maggie Thatcher. However, when recessions come along or when things start to tighten up (such as following 11 September 2001) then businesses that are highly geared (have high borrowing) are generally stuffed. Beware – if you believe that recession is around the corner do not contemplate a highly geared deal. Also note that these businesses can be very vulnerable post-acquisition to more traditionally funded competitors.

Case study

I remember some years ago talking to a kitchen unit manufacturer about competitor analysis. He had been going through a particularly difficult period, with competitors apparently springing up overnight and taking away market share. Just recently a rather more serious competitor had emerged that was threatening his very existence. Realising that he could not ignore this threat he decided to find out more about them. His research was as follows. First of all he asked around about them – customers, competitors, suppliers, his drivers, etc. The word on the street was that this new competitor was an established business but that there had been a recent management buy out. Obviously, with additional funding they were flexing their muscles and trying to buy market share with what my friend called 'silly prices' and other deals. Wondering how big this new war chest was, he decided to do a bit more rooting around. Who had invested in his competitor and how much had they put in?

He went to the business library at Warwick University (which is excellent) and asked the librarian how he could find out more about his competitors. What he discovered was quite amazing. There were financial databases, newspaper extracts, etc – all available on computer. He searched through the national papers to find any articles about this new competitor. Sure enough there was a big article in the financial press about the investment that a venture capital house had made. Reading a bit further he noticed that most of the money had in fact been provided as loans, which as you remember have interest charges. In fact, to my friend's mind the loan repayments looked massive.

The next stage was to dig out their accounts, again using the computer, which showed that over the last few years this business had under-performed and had run up large debts. A quick analysis convinced my friend that a lot of this new money had gone into paying off old creditors and buying out the previous owners. The reality was that only about £50,000 was available to fund an aggressive sales effort – which was what they were now engaged in.

My friend felt that this new intelligence gave him the measure of his new competitor. He decided that some sort of delaying tactics were required to wear out his competitor financially. The plan was to avoid bidding against them at silly non-profitable prices. This meant that if my friend were successful in his tenders he would make some profit (but not much) and that if he lost them to this new competitor he was confident that they were making no profit (because of their increased interest costs).

The battle was protracted, but after about 12 months this competitor suddenly disappeared and the local market settled down again. Reading the newspaper, my friend saw that due to unsustainable losses his competitor had decided to pull out of the market and concentrate their efforts elsewhere. In fact, within a short time after that the business went bust – profit levels were insufficient to fund the high (and getting higher) level of debt.

And a few words on MBIs and BIMBOs

The previous pages have been about MBOs and most of what you have read applies equally to MBIs and BIMBOs. However, a few words will not go amiss in explaining these, although they are really just variants on the concept of buying into a company.

MBI

A management buy-in (MBI) is where a private equity house (venture capitalist) backs an individual to buy into a company and take it over. It is quite common for the private equity house and the buy-in candidate to have some long-term relationship – they have probably backed that person before, and both have done very well out of the deal when previous MBI businesses have sold.

Amtrak

A good example of an MBI was when 3i, the venture capitalist, brought in Mick Jones (previously chief executive of Business Post, a fierce rival to Amtrak) to lead the MBI into Amtrak. Mick Jones had fallen foul of a boardroom coup at Business Post – the semi-retired Kane brothers who owned just over 50 per cent of the company decided to regain operational control. They ousted Jones and sent him on extended gardening leave, presumably to keep him out of harm's way. Bored with playing golf and reading the papers, one day he received a call from 3i, who asked him if he would be interested in leading an MBI into Amtrak. Of course he was. Unknown to Jones, Roger Baines, who owned Amtrak, was looking to sell his stake, valued at around £90 million. He had approached 3i to broker a deal. Probably at that stage they would have been looking at the possibility of a trade sale. However, when they found out that Jones was available an MBI seemed the obvious option, if he was interested. Jones was available, had a perfect track record and industry knowledge – and he was interested. He accepted the offer and the MBI took place.

BIMBO

An unusual name, which stands for 'buy-in management buy-out' and is essentially a combination of an MBI and an MBO. This is where a company's existing management team join up with an incoming managing director backed by a private equity house to acquire the company. For the private equity house this is a 'win-win' situation. They get to put their own person into an established business where there is support from the existing management team.

3. Public market

While many chief executives may secretly dream of taking their business onto the stock market (either full or AIM), it is the least likely exit route for most companies. The main reason for most businesses not going to the public market is either size (too small to make it really worthwhile) or not attractive enough (low profitability and lack of outstanding prospects). Essentially the public market is for high growth/high profit businesses – and even they find it a difficult process. Another consideration is that the public market does not like buying out major shareholders. The argument is that the public market is for raising fresh capital for growth and not for rewarding exiting shareholders. However, it is possible for shareholders to sell some of their equity, but they would be locked in (usually) for a minimum of two years for most of their shareholding. If the initial requirement is for only a few million pounds now and the rest some years down the road, then the public market may be an attractive option if your business is quite large and has continued growth potential.

AIM has already been covered in some detail in Chapter 4 on equity funding. In principle an IPO (initial public offering) on the full Stock Exchange involves much of the same processes. It is, however, worth briefly mentioning some of the reasons for using either AIM or a full listing for an IPO – and some of the drawbacks.

Pros

- Can be the best (and sometimes only) way to raise large amounts of growth funding – it provides where conventional banking falls short. Quoted shares (especially those trading at or near their maximum price) can be issued to fund acquisitions or raise cash for working capital and capital expenditure.

- Can be used (as already mentioned) for partial realisation of investment, ie partial exit of founding shareholders. This may be useful for directors to pay off their mortgages and borrowing against earlier share purchases.

- Can be used to incentivise staff – they can have option schemes for shares of recognisable value and liquidity, ie they are quoted and saleable.

- Can be used to enhance the reputation of the company (and its directors/shareholders) – quoted companies are part of the 'club' and as such there are considerable trading benefits, such as getting onto invitations to tender.

Cons

- The cyclical nature of the market does not reflect the real value of many companies. Since 11 September 2001 many good companies have had depressed share prices – can you imagine how difficult a new share might find it? In the autumn of 2001 there were no main market IPOs (apart from investment trusts) and the number of AIM IPOs was greatly reduced. The FTSE stood at around 5,000 against a high of over 6,700, which reflects a depressed and unloved market place that would not offer full value for some companies coming to the market.

- Size constraints – some companies are just too small to economically raise money this way. There are no real regulatory rules preventing small IPOs, but market practice/economics dictate that the minimum values are as shown in Table 8.3.

Table 8.3 Minimum values for listing

	Capitalisation	**Raising**
Main float	£50 million	£20 million
AIM float	10 million	£3 million

- Regulatory constraints – both the main market and AIM have rules and regulations such as:
  - directors' fiduciary duties;
  - timely announcements of events, eg poor trading news that may affect share price;
  - reporting requirements: full reporting and against tighter timetable (both full and interims);
  - restrictions on directors' dealings: cannot sell shares during 'closed' periods surrounding year-end and half-year results;
  - adviser costs;
  - perceived loss of control;
  - on the main market there are additional constraints, such as: conditions for suitability (must have a three-year track record); shareholders' consents for transactions; financial systems need to be of higher standard.
- Valuation discount – to make it worthwhile for the new investors under an IPO, share floats are normally priced at a discount to the expected ongoing market value to give investors a warm feeling. If similar businesses have had an historic P/E ratio of, say, 14 then a float will go ahead at a P/E of around 11 to offer about a 20 per cent discount to the new shareholders.

- In the public eye – if you are a quoted company the financial world is constantly watching:

  – rules impose a duty to keep the market informed of price-sensitive developments such as poor trading performance, proposed takeovers, etc;

  – analysts will do their own independent research and circulate it to investors, which will have an effect on your share price (unfairly you may think);

  – City investors are often criticised for being too short term.

- Technical/complex process – if you thought that AIM was complicated (see Chapter 4 on equity funding) then an IPO on the main market is horrendous. Table 8.4 gives some idea of the two main processes – technical/regulatory and marketing. The top part of the chart shows the technical and regulatory activities going on during the run-up to D-day (flotation). The bottom part of the chart shows the marketing activities going on at the same time to ensure that the flotation is a success (just nicely oversubscribed will do). Between them runs a time line that shows when these activities typically happen in relation to D-day. I think you will agree that a lot is going on.

- Expensive/time-consuming – obviously the costs will vary according to how much you are trying to raise. However, there is a large element of fixed cost (almost regardless of how much you are raising). Consequently, to all intents and purposes £500,000 is the least it will cost. At the same time your management team are almost fully occupied for up to four months in making sure the flotation succeeds. Don't forget that during this time you also have a business to run.

Why floats succeed or fail

There is an ongoing debate about the success of otherwise of AIM in comparison to the main market. The detractors argue that for most companies AIM does not offer the access to future funding that they had anticipated. At the same time they comment that due to limited availability of shares and control of prices (by company brokers/market makers), there is no real free market in their shares. Some companies that have floated on the main market have argued that despite good trading their shares are selling at a discount – somehow the City does not seem to like them. The truth (as always) is somewhere close to these statements except there is some sort of explanation, which I offer below.

Successful floats:

- The company delivers against its growth expectations – if you do what you say you are going to do the City will like you and reward your share price. As a colleague of mine once said, 'The trick is to under promise and over deliver.' This is mostly correct but do make sure that the 'under promise' is not pitched too low otherwise they will not be too impressed by what you do deliver.

- Success will deliver a growing share price – in the long term, growing profits will lead to a growth in share price, because share prices follow company profitability. In the short term, share prices can be shored up by positive chairman's statements, such as takeover news and new contracts won.

- Success breeds success – if a company consistently delivers good growth in sales and profit this will be rewarded by a high share rating. Any future announcements will trigger a favourable response in the share price – it's almost predictable.

Unsuccessful floats:

- The company disappoints against market expectations – it makes sense that if you don't do what you say, the market will penalise you. The first time you disappoint, the market will give you a slap on the wrist. Persistent disappointment will lead to your share price almost certainly being sidelined – any future good financial news will tend to be ignored for a long time. You will need to re-establish a track record before the share price starts to move again.

- Suddenly your sector goes out of favour – unfair, arguably, but it does happen. Remember the furore as the dotcom bubble burst. All

Table 8.4 Flotation timetable

Technical and Regulatory		
Parties involved: All parties	Reporting accountants/other professionals	All parties
Activity: Scoping meetings	Financial and commercial due diligence Instruct advisors re: employee incentive schemes	Drafting sessions Draft prospectus reviewed by Stock Exchange Legal due diligence Articles/service agreements, etc reviewed
Documentation: Engagement letters Administrative documents	Long form report Short form report Other reports Employee share ownership and bonus scheme	Initial draft prospectus Final form prospectus Stock Exchange comments Final form legal documents
Time line: 15 weeks to go	13 weeks to go	7 weeks to go
Parties involved: Sponsor/ company	Sponsor/broker/company	Sponsor/broker/ company
Activity: Brokers' beauty parade Board structure finalised	Test marketing with potential investors Market identified	Valuation bench-marking Method of float finalised Structure of float finalised
Documentation: Initial market views	Investor feedback	Valuation model
	Marketing	

Source: Ernst & Young

Table 8.4   *Continued*

Technical and Regulatory		
Reporting accountants/sponsor/company/ lawyers company	All parties	Sponsor
Working capital and profit forecast Verification	Completion meeting	Dealings commence
Working capital report	Prospectus	Funds transferred
Profit forecast report	Press release	
Verification notes Pathfinder	Placing agreement Comfort letters/final; reports	
Pathfinder press release		
5 weeks to go	3 weeks to go	D day
Company/sponsor/broker/ financial PR	Broker	Financial PR
Presentation rehearsals	Marketing roadshow	Dealings commence
Employee presentation	Book building and pricing	
Pathfinder circulated to potential investors		
List of potential investors	List of places	Press coverage

Marketing

the dotcom and other similar high tech stocks fell out of favour – even Bill Gates' fortune fell by a billion or so. This was (you may say) unfair because Microsoft was still making good money and yet its share price was depressed due to its sector falling out of favour. Tough – these things happen. The other side of the coin was that traditional shares (construction, engineering, retail) all rose, not because they were suddenly more profitable, but because demand switched to these. It's sort of swings and roundabouts.

● There's no real market for shares, leading to a static share price – this tends to happen to small capitalisation companies (ie those that are not worth very much) because there are very few shares to trade and thus no free market for them. This can be made worse where shares are held by investment trusts and individuals who invested under schemes that gave them tax relief – they will not sell and jeopardise that relief, even though there are underlying pressures that should force the share price upwards.

What about your exit routes?

Before you dismiss the options of MBO, MBI, BIMBO and public market flotation in favour of the trade sale, give them a second thought. The MBO must be a serious option if you have a strong management team with some equity already. Because they already have some equity they may have the stomach for raising some more to get all the business. It is a softer sale and you can help them prepare the case for funding. However, they may not be able to pay as much as a trade buyer. The likelihood is, therefore, that a trade sale is the preferred option – and you probably already know who you can sell it to. The next chapter looks at targeting buyers and packaging the business for sale.

Chapter summary

In this chapter we have looked at the possible exit routes: trade sale, MBI, MBO, BIMBO and public market. For most of you who are reading this book there is only one real option – the trade sale. Don't take this as a personal affront: this is the way most businesses are sold. It's a cheap and fast way to sell businesses. However, if you don't want a complete exit then do consider a public market flotation – it will give you some cash now and (if the company does well) a lot more later. A word of warning: if you do go for a flotation it will totally take you over for some four months or so. Remember that during this time you have a business to run. You need one team dealing with the float and another running the business. This is a good test of your management team and delegation.

As a final word on exit routes – are you ready? Don't start the process until you have squared it with other shareholders (friends and family) and with yourself. Don't forget you only sell your business once, so make sure that you get the best offer. You do not want to haunt yourself forever with the thought, 'Could I have got more?'

9 *Packaging the business*

Make sure all your ducks are lined up

If you own all the shares in your business and operate a virtual dictatorship, then the following words of caution may be of little interest to you. You will just push the button (to sell the business) and get on with it. However, many businesses have a whole raft of stakeholders that need to be taken into consideration.

Controlling shareholders

It is not uncommon for ownership (even of private companies) to become quite widespread over the years. The original founding owner may pass some down to partners and children. In some cases these people might not even be involved in the business – the transfers are done primarily for inheritance tax planning purposes. This can bring a new dynamic to the question of a sale. Technically the person (or persons) who controls 51 per cent of the ordinary shares of a company can sell the business and the rest of the shareholders will be bound by that decision (in most cases). Of course, if there is any evidence of fraud being committed against the minority shareholders then they can put their case to the court.

The objective is to ensure that all the shareholders are singing from the same hymn sheet. You do not want a situation where the majority share-holder, who is negotiating one deal, finds out (as times goes on) that another group of shareholders has become dissatisfied with this deal and started its own negotiations with another party. Ludicrous as this may seem it has happened before – in fact it is quite common practice with public companies. You may have read in the press about 'hostile' takeovers going on where one set of shareholders favours one deal and a second set favours another.

The key to ensuring that all the shareholders are kept in line is to discuss the matter in advance and have a shareholders agreement in place. This written agreement is the evidence you will need to convince a buyer that they are dealing with someone who has the authority to negotiate a deal.

Other shareholders

It may seem obvious, but all shareholders are not the same. What I mean to say is that different groups of shareholders will have different objectives/agendas that need to be understood before a sale can proceed. One particular group of shareholders that you will need to watch out for is venture capital/private equity shareholders. If they own any of the equity in your business you must talk to them first before you start to take any active steps to sell the company. Let me give you a couple of examples.

Case study 1

One of my previous employers was a venture capital fund. In particular we specialised in doing schemes under the Business Expansion Scheme (BES). Under the BES investors got tax relief on their investment (up to 40 per cent in some cases) provided that the investment met certain criteria and that they held their investment for a certain period of time (I think it was four years in those days). We had made an investment in a business (on behalf of our BES investors) and held about 40 per cent of the equity in a privately owned kitchen unit manufacturer.

I would like to say that all was well, but it was not. I was the non-executive director on their board and life was a nightmare. It was a family business and our plan was for the son to succeed the father as managing director. Eventually, after some protracted discussions, this was achieved. However, in the meantime the business ran out of money. The directors, thinking it was a good idea, decided to raise further funding by selling some shares. They proudly announced that they had found a knight in shining armour who would invest £400,000 in return for a significant equity stake.

When I found some more details of the deal I was horrified and had to veto it – despite the company desperately needing the cash. Why was I so intent on blocking the deal? There were two problems for me (and the shareholders that I represented). First, the proposed share issue was on more favourable terms than that which our shareholders had invested in. Essentially, out of desperation the directors wanted to sell these shares at a cheaper price than our shareholders had bought at just six months earlier. I knew that our shareholders would not stomach this loss. The second issue was one of protecting their tax relief, which was more important. By issuing these new shares at this time the company would have breached its tax covenants. Basically this would mean that all our shareholders would lose their 40 per cent tax relief, which was one of the main reasons they had invested. I would have been crucified if I had let this deal go ahead. In fact (horrible though it sounded) my shareholders would have been better off if I had let the company go bust – just as long as I protected their tax relief. As it happens the company did not go bust. I had to negotiate other funding, which did not involve equity.

The moral of this story is: make sure you find out how all your shareholders will react if you sell some or all of the equity. Some may love the idea but others (as in this case) will fight against it.

Case study 2

A friend of mine was managing director (and majority shareholder) of a packaging manufacturer based in Lincolnshire. Some 10 years earlier the company had approached a venture capitalist to help fund its growth aspirations and as a result the venture capitalist acquired 20 per cent of the equity in return for a sizeable cash injection. Over the years the business hit trading troubles, mostly due to the wild fluctuations in the world market of paper prices. Initially the venture capitalist was supportive, but when it became clear that they were not going to get the sort of return they had planned, they lost interest in my friend's company. In effect they became a sleeping partner.

Some years later my friend asked the venture capitalist if they would sell their shares back to the company since it appeared that they were not really interested any more. The response was short – no. When asked for a reason he was not offered anything more tangible than it was not their policy. A few years later a supplier wanted to acquire a 25 per cent stake in my friend's company to forge a strategic alliance. By doing this the supplier hoped to ensure both continuation of trade and growth in the business. The supplier would offer improved credit lines and better prices/availability of product as the business grew. The deal seemed to make sense – to everyone except the venture capitalist. They said no, and had the power to do so under their subscription agreement.

It seemed to my friend that he was locked into the venture capitalist forever with no apparent way out. The relationship had broken down. Some time later the venture capitalist appointed a new non-executive director to look after this investment. My friend spent some time discussing the situation with them and they agreed to sell the shares back to the company. Why the sudden change in policy? Time moves on, people move on (especially in venture capitalist businesses), etc. They had at last accepted that the investment had failed to meet the original objective (high capital growth/payback) and that any return was now preferable to close the matter.

The moral of this story is similar to the earlier one: be aware that minority shareholders, especially venture capitalists, can virtually control your business and will block any share sales unless it suits them.

Significant stakeholders

The final group of people that you have to consider are those that do not even own any shares in your business, but in fact make up your business entirely – employees, suppliers and customers. You must consider how they will react to a sale. If there is any fallout from any of these then you do not have a business to sell – and due diligence will uncover it. Let's briefly look at each in turn.

Employees

Key employees must be kept on board. If they walk then you may not be able to sell the company, or the price at which you do sell will be greatly reduced. In many cases it is uncertainty that worries employees. Put their minds at rest – tell them that whoever buys the business will be vetted to ensure that it is 'business as usual'. You may want to offer key employees favourable employment contracts that ensure that they get 6 to 12 months' salary if the worst comes to the worst. You will also keep them on board by talking to them early on in the process and incentivising them. Don't give them shares (you don't need another minority group), but give them bonuses tied into the successful sale of the business. Be open with them and tell them what is going on – they are not stupid. A client of mine who sold up last year did not tell the assistant accountant why I was there (I was there to prepare the information memorandum prior to sale). There should have been a cover story to the effect that I was reviewing information systems/financial performance. He nearly sussed why I was there – a close shave!

Customers

Have you considered how they might react if you sold the company, especially to a competitor? Obviously, in grooming (Chapter 7) we looked at making sure that contracts are in place, but this may not be appropriate for your industry. Some customers may be openly hostile to a transfer of ownership – they may dread your company being owned by a competitor.

This may lead to their getting a worse deal (in their eyes). They may well have left this competitor to come to you. You can't ask your customers for their permission, but you should review your key customers to see how they will respond. If they walk either before or after the sale, this will affect the sale price – especially if any of the purchase price is profit-dependent over subsequent years. You need to 'sell' the deal to customers. Emphasise the benefits to them.

Suppliers

There will similar concerns among this group. They will react a bit like your employees. How will things change for them if the company is sold? A bigger company may want bigger suppliers – this may mean the smaller suppliers will be frozen out. Key suppliers will still be key suppliers to the new owners: find a way to tie them in.

I guess the decision to sell the company has to be run past a lot more people than just the majority shareholder. However, at the end of the day it is your business and so long as you are sensitive to the other parties involved then you can and should have your way. Just remember that to get this (at the price that you want), a few little sweeteners will be needed along the way.

Where will the buyer come from?

When you first decide that you want to sell the business you may well have no idea where the eventual buyer will come from. Well, think again, because you probably do – but you just don't know it yet. Most of my clients engage me to help them groom and sell their business and then ask the same question. I take them through a process that lets them identify where the buyer will come from using the following criteria.

Markets

A buyer may come from your existing market (that much you probably already know). This is frequently referred to as 'horizontal integration' and the potential buyer will usually be a competitor – but they may come from another market altogether. The same principles of cost saving, competition reduction, capturing a larger market, etc apply to other businesses not necessarily in your direct market.

In 'vertical integration' a company obtains control of a supplier to achieve these advantages. This means that you could target a customer who is looking to move further down the supply chain, to improve value added. Alternatively, you could look for a supplier who is also looking at vertical integration, but this time moving up the supply chain. They may all be possibilities, which means you have already increased the list.

Products or services

This is not necessarily a duplication of markets, above. You should try and identify other businesses that offer complementary products or services. I knew of a business that made aftermarket alloy wheels for cars. It had exhausted the search for direct competitors. It eventually found another company that sold other aftermarket products (service parts, body panels, batteries, etc), which was not a supplier, customer or competitor. It wanted to strengthen its position by extending its product range.

Size

Your size is important and will dictate who may want to buy you. It's all to do with visibility and the relative sizes of you and your buyer. Large public companies are constantly looking for businesses to buy (you may remember my observations in the last chapter). However, their radar seldom looks below £10 million; ie if your company is valued at less than this they will not be interested in you. Nothing personal, but it is not worth their time to do this kind of deal. On the other hand, there are masses of smaller companies (AIM or privately owned) that are looking to acquire companies worth up to £5 million. Use this to help you focus on buyers.

Location

It sounds logical: if your business is based in the Midlands then chances are another Midlands business will buy it, especially if your customers are predominantly in that area. This will improve control of the two businesses and may give some operational improvements. If you are a national business based in the Midlands then the possibilities are a bit wider. There's a chance that a business based in the south will buy as part of its geographical expansion. Of course the operational control issues will need resolving. At an even more local level, especially in retail, a competitor may buy you because your site is better placed than theirs, especially if you have a better/bigger primary location and they have a poorer secondary location. When targeting buyers do not ignore the location factor – look close to home.

Reputation

This will enable you to command the maximum 'goodwill' payment. This can be as a result of your profitable customer base, staff expertise, product or service (brand), etc. Of course you want to mirror this in the companies that you target or at least find one that will value this. For example, you may be ISO 9001 registered – chances are that your buyer will be similar to you. Don't waste your time looking for the cheap and cheerful competitors. I always say to my clients that they should look for a business that they would like to be like – just bigger. If they do, then they have probably found the right partner to buy them.

Ok, by now I hope you have enough pointers to get you looking in the right direction.

Case study

When my friends Jim and Steve were looking to sell their business they set about carefully targeting buyers. They realised that they had a very special business: it was the biggest privately owned company involved in chemical testing and monitoring of contaminated land, ground water leachates and landfill gas in the UK; all the rest had already been bought up. The obvious choice was a trade sale to a competitor – but who? Jim had excellent knowledge of the market place: he was a mover and shaker and knew everyone. A large trade buyer, preferably quoted or with venture capital backing, would be needed – they could afford a decent price. Another quality company or someone that recognised their quality was required, which ruled out a handful of companies. What about location? How relevant would that be in the equation? Very relevant – they could identify several major players that did not have a substantial presence in the Midlands. A final factor they considered was who was already active in acquiring companies. It was important to find an experienced buyer (they would know what to do) not a virgin buyer who might get cold feet.

The result of Jim's targeting brought up a short list of two companies – one UK-based (a quoted plc) and the other a Dutch plc (with venture capital backing). It was down to Jim to package the company as well as he could for one (or both) of these buyers.

Getting to the buyers

Of course many of you will not be as fortunate as Jim and Steve – you don't know the exact identity of your buyer. This means that you will need some further help to locate the company that fits the criteria that you have selected. There are three recognised ways of locating buyers – let's call them candidates.

Advertising

You will find businesses for sale in a wide range of daily and weekly publications. These include *Daltons Weekly* and *Exchange and Mart,* which are good for retail businesses, and the broadsheets such as the *Telegraph, The Times* and *Financial Times,* which are good for manufacturing and service businesses. In addition you will find trade-specific publications that also include adverts for businesses for sale. You will also find businesses for sale via the Internet. Two sites that I have visited are, first, www. companiesforsale.uk.com, which is run by the accountants Grant Thornton. This site is suitable for both buyers and sellers – buyers will be e-mailed suitable companies that meet their declared criteria (industry, turnover, etc). I looked at a couple of the businesses – summary financial information, number of employees, principal activities, key strengths of business, and location. My feeling was that the information looked as if it had been lifted directly from an information memorandum – the numerical section headings were a dead giveaway. If you subscribe and sign up to its confidentiality agreement you will receive fuller details on companies for sale.

The other site is www.business-sale.com, established in 1995. The Business Sale Report offers businesses for sale in the UK and Europe, information on which it receives from business brokers, accountants and private sellers. It also monitors trade press and receives details through its site. It seemed to offer a listing, which had minimal details. Again, if you subscribe and sign up to its confidentiality agreement you will receive fuller details on companies for sale.

Direct mail

Another method is to approach buyers and intermediaries directly. This involves creating your own database of candidates and sending them a brief overview of your company for sale (an executive summary will do), inviting them to contact you directly for the information memorandum (subject to signing a confidentiality agreement). The challenge is in creating the database of candidates, although you may recall in the last chapter how my kitchen unit manufacturer used the excellent library at Warwick University to dig out financial and press articles on companies. Finding appropriate intermediaries is a bit easier to do: they are listed in directories, and your Business Link may also be able to help you.

Personal approach

My preferred option would be to choose a trusted or recommended intermediary. This could be your accountant or solicitor, or someone who they or a trusted business friend might suggest. This way you are dealing with one person who knows your business and the type of buyer you are looking for, has a reputation to protect, and will only put forward to you companies that they know to be worthwhile. In effect a lot of the filtering has been done for you. Make sure you tell them which companies you do not want them to approach – there may be some sensitivities. The end result is, hopefully, one or more companies that want to find out more about your company.

Of course there is a lot that you can do yourself to try and target buyers. If you are good at networking then this is where you can find buyers. Join business clubs, your local Chamber of Commerce, Business Link, your trade organisation, go to your bank/accountants/stockbrokers' seminars. These are fertile ground for people that want to do business.

Marketing the business

The objective is to make contact with the principal, ie a buyer. However, sometimes you have to work through an intermediary. Don't be put off: there are many good reasons for buyers appointing an intermediary. They may be serial buyers of businesses (this is good news as far as you are concerned) and to speed things up they use an intermediary to filter the possibilities. There is another advantage to dealing with an intermediary, especially if you are using one as well: it takes out some of the angst of the negotiating. I don't know what you are like at negotiating and how well you respond when the person you are negotiating with says no to your proposals. It is far easier if you can say to your adviser something like, 'Ask him if they will pay £15 million for the business and the net assets on a £ per £ basis.' Your intermediary then talks directly to their intermediary and a dialogue/negotiation begins. This can continue without your involvement – left in the hands of professionals who understand the nuances of this type of situation. They don't get upset by blunt responses, which might appear insulting to you. It's all part of the ritual, which ultimately will lead to the basis of a deal or none at all. You can get on with running your business, without this distraction.

Ultimately you have to prepare a document that packages up your company into something that your targeted buyer wants. This document is called an 'information memorandum', and it is an important part of marketing your business.

Information memorandum

This is arguably the most important document in the sale process. It is the company's 'shop window' and the quality of this document alone may well determine whether a prospective buyer makes an offer or not, especially if they do not have any first-hand knowledge of your business. The information memorandum is not dissimilar to a business plan in that it contains information on the company background, history to date, details of products/

services, employees and financial information. Its key purpose is to demonstrate the level of maintainable profits that the company is capable of generating. Ideally the business should already have stripped out all the excess proprietorial costs in arriving at these profits, ie excess salaries (partners/other non-essential directors), excess pension contributions, car costs, etc. Obviously the higher the maintainable earnings, the higher the price the business will fetch. Don't forget that at a P/E multiple of 10, £100,000 of extra maintainable profits is worth another £1 million on the selling price. So it's worth the effort.

I would suggest that your information memorandum should contain the following headings:

- Executive summary – a brief one or two-page summary of the company that 'sells' the business. It is the 'hook' that gets the reader to buy into what follows. It should be punchy and to the point:

  - what the company does;

  - summary of main financial information highlighting maintainable earnings;

  - key strengths of the company;

  - future development and growth opportunities.

- Introduction – sets the scene and lays down some basic factual information:

  - description of the company;

  - ownership details;

  - auditors, solicitors, bankers, etc;

  - opportunities for the company;

  - reason for sale.

- Company history and development – this is the brief history of the business, with key dates and events highlighted:

  - how and when the company started;

- milestones in the development of the company;

- key changes of ownership;

- background to the industry.

- Current operations – gives details of how and where the business is carried out and some market information:

  - location;

  - description of operations (capacity, services offered, etc);

  - analysis of market and competition;

  - main customers (don't mention names).

- Management and employees – gives details of the key employees that represent the main skills and management base of the business. It is vital to demonstrate that the company is well managed and has the right people for the future:

  - analysis of employees (don't mention names);

  - CVs for key employees (including directors).

- Assets – gives details of the key assets that the company has. It is important that these demonstrate state of the art and capability. You don't want to show a picture of a rundown business needing major investment. If there is a property included then show a recent valuation:

  - summary of net book value by key fixed asset grouping;

  - significant assets.

- Financial information – I am not too prescriptive about the format and content for this. However, you do need to give some historic performance over at least the previous two years. If there are significant variations in performance over this period, eg a drop in gross margin or sales, then you should provide some commentary on why this occurred. The objective is to show that it is non-recurring (if negative) or will continue (if positive):

- – summary of trading results highlighting maintainable earnings;

- – summary of forecasts.

- Arrangements for offers – it is important that you lay down the ground rules for making offers and how investigations will be conducted. You do not want a careless visiting 'suit' upsetting staff with their questions, and worse still giving the game away. This nearly happened to one of my clients when a junior accountant questioned why I needed certain information – there had been no prior briefing (obviously with a smokescreen story):

  - – deadline for offers and where to submit them;

  - – arrangements for visits and negotiations (on or off site/announcements).

- Caveats – this document is for limited use only: it is not a public memorandum. You should state that the directors have taken all reasonable steps to check for accuracy and that the document is for private use, ie they cannot give to others and cannot be relied on for making a financial commitment.

- Appendices – obviously these will vary from company to company but should include things like brochures, copies of accounts and other significant documents.

An example of an information memorandum

The above guidelines were incorporated in an information memorandum that I prepared in 2001 to help one of my clients successfully sell their business – Jim and Steve (I have mentioned them in earlier chapters). It is reproduced in the Appendix to this chapter. I do not hold it out as a perfect example, although it did work very well for them. The company that bought them commented on the quality of the document, which was very gratifying for all concerned. I have tried to disguise the document so some of the detail may look a little strange; while I know that they do not mind me using them as a case study, they do not want every detail to be blatantly displayed. There are some details that are very specific to their situation (and that of their buyer). I have also left out the executive summary and the appendices. We aimed this document specifically at this buyer – you can say we targeted them and pitched the sale squarely at them. You should do the same.

Just a few quick words on the information memorandum in the Appendix. It follows the format that I suggested above, but there were just a couple of points that were specific to this business.

As you can imagine the buyer that they targeted to buy the company made their own request for information – buyers do this. Rather than reply directly to this they made sure that the information memorandum answered all the queries. This information request is referred to in the document and a copy enclosed in the appendices.

The forecasts were prepared to reflect two situations – no growth and growth. The purpose of the forecasts is obviously to 'hook' the buyer into paying more for a company that shows greater potential than has been delivered. The most optimistic forecast (growth) showed maintainable profit of £1.95 million for a business that had only made £534,000 in its last full year.

The use of 'earnings before interest and tax' (EBIT) is to make the measure of profit look bigger. It excludes interest and tax and is the preferred measure for large corporate buyers.

A final word of advice. You've heard the expression, 'Don't teach your grandmother how to suck eggs.' In your information, and any other written correspondence, do not include a price that you want for the company, and do not suggest to your buyer how to value your company. They know how to value a company – they have probably done so several times before. Let them suggest a price, and make appropriate noises when they do.

Confidentiality

You will have noticed that reference has been made to a confidentiality agreement. It is absolutely essential that before you reveal too much sensitive information (and I include the information memorandum in this) you get all parties receiving it to sign up to the confidentiality agreement. Basically this restricts the distribution and use of this information. The following confidentiality agreement is the one I offered to Jim and Steve.

Confidentiality Agreement

PERSONAL AND CONFIDENTIAL

Name:

Company:

Address:

Date:

Dear

This is to confirm the interest of *(insert name of company)* in examining the business of ABC plc ('the company') for the sole purpose of evaluating the company with a view to the acquisition of that company. In connection with such examination you will be provided with certain financial statements and other information and documents relating to the company and its business. In consideration of the conduct of such examination, *(insert name of company)* will keep in strict confidence and will not, directly or indirectly, divulge i) the fact that such an examination is being conducted, or ii) any of the financial and other information provided by us to you.

(Insert name of company) acknowledges that documents provided to you by us contain confidential information that will at all times remain the exclusive property of the company. You further acknowledge that you will be responsible for the safekeeping of these documents and will not reproduce, disseminate or otherwise disclose the information contained therein to any third parties. Upon receipt of a written demand from the company you will return these documents to the company together with any copies in your possession or that of your advisers.

You acknowledge that the company would sustain irreparable damage in the event of a breach of this agreement by *(insert name of company)*.

Accordingly, in the event of any such breach, the company will be entitled to seek and obtain immediate injunctive relief against *(insert name of company)*. This agreement will be binding on *(insert name of company)*, its employees, directors and representatives.

This agreement is governed by and shall be construed in accordance with English Law.

Yours faithfully

ABC plc
Name:
Position:

(Insert name of company)
Name:
Position:
Date:

What about your packaging?

At this stage you must be really serious about selling your business. You should have finally established the selling price, ie what you want for your baby. Your packaging has got to support this price. Start getting all the information together now, both for the information memorandum and due diligence that will follow. Start thinking about how you want to be paid – cash, shares, etc. The next chapter looks at the final stages of selling the company and the various ways in which the buyer might offer to pay you.

Chapter summary

In this chapter we have looked at preparing the business for sale – targeting buyers and packaging the business. Chances are that you already have a pretty good idea of who will buy your business – usually a competitor, customer or even supplier. Hopefully I have given you some more ideas on where your buyer may be and how you can get to them. Your information memorandum is your selling tool, which you will send to serious buyers. Do make sure that you make a good job of this vital document.

Apart from grooming, this is the most important stage in selling your business. Time spent here will reap greater rewards later. My feeling is that while you have all the information to hand, seek advice on preparing the information memorandum. You usually only get one bite at the cherry, so get this bit right to get the maximum price for your business.

Appendix: an example of an information memorandum

ABC plc

(Registered in England and Wales No xxxxxxxxxx)

Information Memorandum

Prepared by the Directors

Contents

Section   Heading

Executive Summary
1.   Introduction
2.   Company History and Development
3.   Current Operations
4.   Management and Employees
5.   Assets
6.   Financial Information
7.   Arrangements for Offers
8.   Caveats

Appendices:

Appendix 1: Audited Accounts y/e 31st December 1999
Appendix 2: Draft Accounts (unaudited) y/e 31st December 2000
Appendix 3: Information Request

Executive Summary

What the company does
Summary of main financial information highlighting maintainable earnings
Key strengths of the company
Future development and growth opportunities

1. Introduction

Description of the company
ABC plc (ABC) specialises in the chemical testing and monitoring of contaminated land, ground water leachates and landfill gas. The company is UKAS Accredited and takes part in a number of proficiency testing schemes. As a result of involvement with the European Standards Committee (CEN) ABC has been contracted to assist in setting up and participating in a European exercise to validate a number of draft European Standards concerned with the analysis of waste. The company has been a NVQ awarding centre since April 1999, and in February 2000 the company achieved Investor in People status.

The company first embarked on the xxxxxx Excellence Model some four years ago. Under this business model the company's performance is benchmarked against other companies over a wide range of measures. It has recently made its submission to the 2001 xxxxxx Excellence Awards.

Ownership
ABC converted to plc status in April 1997. The authorised and issued share capital is £50,000. The ownership of these is split as follows:

Jim xxxxxx   £25,500 (51%)
Steve xxxxxx   £24,500 (49%)

The full time directors of the company are:

Jim xxxxxx (Chairman)
Steve xxxxxx (Managing Director)
xxxxxxx (Finance Director and Company Secretary)
xxxxxxx (Quality Director)

Auditors, solicitors and bankers
(Obviously you would include their full address – I have excluded this detail.)

Auditors:
BDO Stoy Hayward

Solicitor:
Brindley, Twist, Tafft & James

Bankers:
Barclays Bank plc

Lloyds TSB Commercial Finance Limited

Opportunities for the company
The company has forecasted that over the course of the next 1 year sales will increase by x% to £xxx with associated maintainable EBIT of £xxx. This can be delivered from the current premises with some additional investment in automated equipment and staff. The directors hold the view that the company is well placed to achieve the sales growth both through its own growing reputation and as a result of the market growth brought about by current and future UK and European legislation.

In addition, to the organic growth of its laboratory in xxxxxxx, the company plans to establish laboratories within two key strategic geographic areas in the UK over the next 18 months. The contribution to turnover and profit from these centres has not been included in the above figures as detailed projections have not been formulated.

Reason for sale
The company has achieved considerable success to date, which it is confident can be sustained. Over the last 12 months the directors have been aware of a consolidation within their market sector, which has led to a reduction in independent companies like their own. In response to several direct approaches by larger companies both within and outside this sector the directors have decided to respond to these. Whilst it is hoped that a sale can take place that will maximise shareholder value this is by no means the only course of action open to the company. Should no sale take place the directors will continue to drive the company forward in line with the projections referred to above.

2. Company History and Development

How and when the company started
ABC Limited was incorporated in August 1985 and commenced trading in February 1986 on the University of xxxxxxx Science Park. Originally owned and managed by the original founders Jim xxxxxx and John xxxxxx by 1987 Jim xxxxxx had acquired sole ownership of the company. The company was set up to capitalise on the newly established contamination analysis market.

Milestones in the development of the company
The company moved to larger premises at xxxxxx in 1991. Within 12 months the company had grown to such an extent that an additional unit was acquired. During 1995 and 1997 further growth led to the company acquiring yet additional units at xxxxxx.

In December 2000 the company moved to its current premises at xxxxxx. The importance of this move is that it enabled the company to consolidate all its operations on one site and have the potential for future growth without the need for further relocation.

The company is proud to have been associated with a number of major civil engineering projects in the UK, such as: Canary Wharf, Second Severn Bridge, Channel Tunnel, Jubilee Line extension.

At the time, the company located at xxxxxx had 13 employees, and has now grown to nearer 100 at the current location.

Key changes of ownership
The original issued share capital in 1985 was £100, which was enlarged in 1997 to £50,000 as a consequence of the company acquiring plc status. In 1990 an external investor (xxxxxx) acquired a 25% stake in the company, which was bought back by the company in 1993. Over the course of the period 1995 to 1997 Jim xxxxxx made share transfers to Steve xxxxxx, which increased his share holding from 25% to the current holding of 49%.

Background to the industry
The entire contamination analysis and remedial market is comparatively new. It has only achieved real significance in the UK within the last 20 years. Over this time event in the UK, Europe and the USA have been instrumental in

new legislation being enacted to enforce additional responsibilities on the owners and users of land. Recent examples of legislation and policy illustrating how the industry is likely to develop in the future are:

- The Government's policy on brown-field sites;
- The EU Landfill Directive;
- The Government's recent draft strategy on waste disposal and recycling;
- The Environment Agency's implementation of the IPPC Directive;
- Draft Statutory Guidance to local authorities on the implementation of Section 57 of the Environmental Protection Act 1996;
- Revisions of BS DD175 and BS 5930, both of which are concerned with the investigation of contaminated sites;
- The DETR Contaminated Land Report, CLR11, which sets out model procedures for the investigation of contaminated sites.

ABC plc has been consulted on the content of BS DD175, BS 5930 and CLR11 and has provided a number of comments that have been incorporated into the final versions. All of the above indicate that further growth in the contamination analysis sector is inevitable.

It is difficult to acquire any other indisputable figures for each of the two constituent parts (analysis and remedial) as these are frequently lumped together. However, the directors believe that based on their own assessment their market place will grow sufficiently to meet their company growth aspirations, either through overall UK market growth or through securing business from their poorer performing competitors.

3. Current Operations

Location

As stated previously the company has consolidated all its operations on one site at xxxxxx. This site currently offers very flexible accommodation with much of the area usable for most purposes. Currently the 26,500 sq ft site is used as follows:

Laboratory space	9,000 sq ft
Sample preparation and storage	4,000 sq ft
Office space	13,500 sq ft

In addition there is currently off-road parking for 50 cars.

There is heating throughout the building and cool air circulation throughout much of the building. In addition, air conditioning is supplied to the ICPMS and organics laboratories and both the chairman and managing directors' offices. All areas are in good decorative order.

The site is currently occupied on a 20-year full tenant-repairing lease at an annual rental of £85,000 exclusive of rates and insurances with five-yearly rental reviews. This lease was granted in March 2001.

Description of operations (capacity, services offered, etc)

(See appendix 3, Information Request, for additional information.)

Currently the company can process 10,000–11,000 (operational capacity) samples per month based on an average mix of determinations. This equates approximately to an annual turnover of about £5 million. However, there is a current plan to increase this by 25% over the next six to eight months. This would increase sample capacity to 13,000 samples per month on the same basis and equate to annual turnover of about £6.5 million. The directors believe that with further automation and staffing the current site has a maximum capacity in the region of 16,000–20,000 samples per month equating to an annual turnover of about £8 to 10 million (at current day prices).

The company has recently improved sample turnaround from an industry average of 10 days to an average of 7 days with approximately 75–80% of its throughput being processed in 5 days or less.

The company offers the following services:

- Metals analysis using one of three ICP-OES instruments or to sub-ppm levels using ICP-MS.
- Organics analysis for a range of determinands using GC/FID, GC/ECD, GC/MS (all with a range of sample introduction techniques), HPLC/UVF, HPLC/Fluorescence, HPLC/ECD and HPLC/DAD.
- A wide range of wet chemical techniques for the determination of ammonia, chloride, cyanide, nitrate, nitrite, phenol, sulphate, sulphide, etc.
- In-situ monitoring and sampling of landfill gas, leachates, groundwater, etc.

Analysis of market place and competition
(See appendix 3, Information Request, for additional information.)

The company's customers are diverse and fall into five main categories:

- Consulting Engineers
- Local Authorities
- Civil Engineering and Land Reclamation Contractors
- Geotechnical Investigation Companies
- Others – builders, consultants, etc.

An outline of the top 10 customers is shown in the appendices.

Key factors are price, quality and service. The company operates in a competitive market place but still manages to provide excellent service and high levels of quality. The company, however, believes that with the consolidation of the competition, and increased workload that prices will stabilise and over the next twelve to eighteen months increase. It is believed that increases in the order of 15–20% over the next three years are not unrealistic. Such strengthening in prices has not been allowed for within the projections presented.

A review of the company's main competitors just over 18 months ago highlighted seven main competitors:

- Competitor 1
- Competitor 2

- Competitor 3
- Competitor 4
- Competitor 5
- Competitor 6
- Competitor 7

As of today as a result of consolidation in the industry this would be reduced to just two companies:

- Competitor 3
- Competitor 5

Throughout the period 1996 to 1999 (the period covered by the February 2001 Environmental Testing report published by Merlin Scott Associates Limited) ABC plc out-performed the industry average in many of the financial criteria measured. Gross Margin Percentage was typically twice the industry average, as was Operating Profit Percentage. Both Return on Capital Employed and Return on Investment were also two to three times the industry average.

4. Management and Employees

Analysis of employees
As of 26 June 2001 there were 98 company employees. They can be classified as follows:

Administration	4	
Finance	3	
Sales and Marketing	11	(including 1 part time)
External Operations	5	
ICP Metals	4	
Logistics	18	
Organics	10	
Quality Control	2	
Sample Preparation	6	
Technical	1	
Water Laboratory	6	
Wet Laboratory	20	(including 3 part time)
Maintenance	1	(part time)
Senior Managers	3	
Directors	4	

All the above are permanent staff although the company does employ a number of students on a temporary basis. The numbers of temporary staff change depending on workload and summer holiday cover required.

CVs for key employees (including directors)

Jim xxxxxx – Chairman
Age xx

Qualifications: Royal Society of Health Diploma in Air Pollution Control; Diploma in Acoustics and Noise Control; ONC in Physical Sciences; HNC in Chemistry

Membership of professional bodies: Fellow of the Royal Society of Chemistry; Chartered Chemist; European Chemist; Member of the Institution of Environmental Sciences; Member of the Institute of Acoustics

Jim is actively involved in numerous committees and working groups both within and outside the industry. Previously worked for xxxxxx, Competitor 5 prior to founding ABC in 1986.

xxxxx xxxxxx – Managing Director
Age xx

Qualifications: BSc (Honours) Engineering Geology and Geotechnics

Membership of professional bodies: Chartered Engineer; Member of the Institution of Civil Engineers; Member of the Institute of Mining and Metallurgy

xxxxxxx previously worked for xxxxxx Limited and Exploration Associates (now part of xxxxxx) prior to joining ABC in 1993 as Operations Director. In 1997 he was appointed Managing Director.

xxxxxx – Finance Director
Age xx

Qualifications: Fellow member of Chartered Association of Certified Accountants

xxxxxx worked in the profession before setting up his own consultancy in 1991. Joined ABC in 1993 having previously worked for the company as a consultant.

xxxxxx – Quality Director
Age xx

Qualifications: Graduate, Royal Society of Chemistry; MSc Analytical Techniques; Chartered Chemist

Membership of professional bodies: Fellow, Chartered Institute of Water and Environmental Management; Fellow of the Royal Society of Chemistry

xxxxxx worked for xxxxxx and xxxxxx prior to joining ABC in 1996 as Quality Manager. In 2000 he was appointed Quality Director.

xxxxxx – Technical Manager
Age xx

Qualifications: Chartered Chemist

Membership of professional bodies: Fellow of the Royal Society of Chemistry

xxxxxx worked for xxxxxx and xxxxxx prior to joining ABC in 1997 as Technical Manager.

xxxxxx – Business Development Manager
Age xx

Qualifications: BSc (Eng) Civil Engineering

Membership of professional bodies: Member of the General Committee of the British Drilling Association; Chairman of Ground Investigation Sub-Committee

xxxxxx has worked within the industry for companies such as xxxxxx and xxxxxx before joining ABC in 1999.

xxxxxx – External Operations Manager
Age xx

Qualifications: BSc Honours Environmental Science; Post Graduate Diploma Environmental Assessment and Monitoring; MSc Environmental Assessment and Monitoring

Membership of professional bodies: Member of the Institution of Environmental Sciences

xxxxxx has worked for ABC since 1990 and was appointed External Operations Manager in 1997.

5. Assets

Summary of net book value by key fixed asset grouping
As at 31 May 2001 the fixed assets were as shown below:

Fixed Assets Summary as at 31 May 2001

	Cost	Accum. Deprec'n	Net Book Value
Property Improvements	151,549	20,298	131,251
Laboratory Equipment	1,207,930	693,371	514,559
Office Equipment	219,034	171,578	47,456
Computer Equipment	130,733	32,652	98,081
Site Monitoring Equipment	88,786	20,346	68,440
Motor Vehicles	115,915	35,419	80,496
DTI Grant	−60,000	0	−60,000
Total	1,853,947	973,664	880,283

Significant assets
The company has the following significant assets:

IT
Hewlett-Packard NetServer LC 3 running Windows NT Server
60 PCs running Windows 95/98/NT Workstation/2000 Pro
34 Printers

Chromatography
2 Hewlett-Packard 1050 HPLC
4 Hewlett-Packard 1100 HPLC
4 Hewlett-Packard 6890 GCs, 3with HP 5973MSDs
3 Hewlett-Packard 5980 GCs
1 Varian Star 3400 with SPME
1 Chrompack CP2002P
1 Dionex DX-100 IC
1 Dionex DX-120 IC

Spectroscopy
1 Thermo Jarrel Ash Atomscan 16 ICP/OES
1 Thermo Jarrel Ash ICAP 61E ICP/OES
1 Perkin Elmer Optima ICP/OES
1 Perkin Elmer Elan ICP/MS
1 Konilab 60 Discrete Analyser

6. Financial Information

Summary of trading results for the last two financial years, highlighting maintainable earnings

Audited accounts for the year to 31st December 1999 and draft audited accounts for the year to 31st December 2000 are included in this document as appendices 1 and 2. The profit and loss statements are summarised below together with the adjustments made to show maintainable earnings.

Summary last two years profit and loss accounts to 31st December

	1999	2000
Sales	**2,253,523**	**3,033,202**
Cost of sales	339,089	650,212
Gross profit	1,914,434	2,382,990
Admin expenses	1,801,756	1,978,382
	112,678	404,608
Other operating income	42,000	0
Operating profit	154,678	404,608

Adjustments to arrive at maintainable profits:

(1) Relocation costs		17,869
(2) Chairman costs	102,654	101,344
(3) Factoring charges	9,007	10,126

Maintainable EBIT	266,339	533,947
Summary of key ratios:		
No. of samples	43,414	67,945
Average sample price	£51.91	£44.64
GP%	84.95%	78.56%
Sales growth	4.06%	34.60%
Maintainable EBIT %	11.82%	17.60%

During the year to 31st December 2000 there were significant cost increases in the glassware used to transport samples for a major customer. In addition delivery and collection costs and sub contract costs were disproportionately higher. At the same time the average price per sample fell by some 14% over the previous year. Together these factors account for the reduction in gross profit to 78.56% (year 2000) compared to 84.95% (year 1999).

Summary of management accounts for the last two years to 30th June 2001

As of today's date the company has management accounts for the first 5 months to 31st May 2001. At this stage the directors have decided to include an estimate for the month of June based on actual sales revenues and estimated running costs based on current performance. To give an indication of the last two complete years trading performance the following profit and loss statement summaries to 30th June have been prepared.

Summary of last two years management accounts to 30th June

	Actual 12 mths to 30/06/2000	Estimated * 12 mths to 30/06/2001
Sales	**2,561,587**	**3,696,264**
Cost of sales	411,618	721,775
Gross profit	2,149,969	2,974,489
Admin expenses	1,842,624	2,439,782
	307,345	534,707
Other operating income	0	0
Operating profit	307,345	534,707
Adjustments to arrive at maintainable profits:		
(1) Relocation costs	0	26,684
(2) Chairman costs	96,465	111,483
(3) Loss on sale of car	0	6,355
(4) Factoring charges	9,000	10,150
Maintainable EBIT	**412,810**	**689,379**
Summary of key ratios:		
No. of samples	52,503	83,512
Average sample price	£48.79	£44.26
GP%	83.93%	80.47%
Sales Growth	n/a	44.30%
Adjusted EBIT %	16.12%	18.65%

Note: * Actual figures for the 11 months to May 2001, estimate for June 2001.

Whilst some £26,684 has been identified as relocation costs it is highly probable that additional costs relating to the relocation have not been identified and have been included within general repairs.

Throughout January and February 2001 sample numbers were held back at 6,379 and 6,241 respectively in preparation for the move from xxxxxx and xxxxxx to xxxxxx. In addition during March the company was paying rental on the old site whilst paying rent on the new site.

Summary of forecasts for the year to 30th June 2001 together with key assumptions

It is anticipated that the sales growth shown above will continue. As an illustration, however, the company has presented below a cautious approach by way of presenting a forecast for the year ended 30th June 2002. It is based on the company continuing to perform at least as well as shown during the period March – June 2001 (four months) management accounts. This is the period since the move to the current premises. It was believed that to include the results for January and February 2001 would not have shown a fair picture – for the reasons outlined in the previous section. During that period the company was operating at the old premises with restricted output. On this basis a pessimistic forecast with no growth for the year to 30th June 2002 is as follows.

Non growth forecast year to 30th June 2002

	2002
Sales	**4,273,226**
Cost of sales	824,157
Gross profit	3,449,068
Admin expenses	2,619,302
	829,766
Other operating income	0
Operating profit	829,766
Adjustments to arrive at maintainable profits	
(1) Relocation costs	0
(2) Chairman costs	122,633
(3) Factoring charges	9,000
Maintainable EBIT	**961,399**
Summary of key ratios	
No. of samples	95,199
Average sample price	£44.89
GP%	80.71%
Sales growth	15.61%
Maintainable EBIT %	22.50%

This forecast is the minimum that the directors believe the company will achieve. It includes some capital expenditure of £100,000, which will occur in August 2001 and is required to provide extra capacity.

A more realistic forecast, based on the growth targeted by the management team in line with the previous growth, would show a performance more in line with the forecast shown below.

Continued growth forecast year to 30th June 2002

	2002
Sales	**5,594,464**
Cost of sales	1,097,085
Gross profit	4,497,379
Admin expenses	2,672,504
	1,824,875
Other operating income	0
Operating profit	1,824,875

Adjustments to arrive at maintainable profits

(1) Relocation costs	0
(2) Chairman costs	122,633
(3) Factoring charges	9,000
Maintainable EBIT	**1,956,508**

Summary of key ratios

No. of samples	126,400
Average sample price	£44.26
GP%	80.39%
Sales growth	51.35%
Maintainable EBIT %	34.97%

It is anticipated that to achieve the above profitability the company will need to continue its reliance on the senior management team. It is therefore envisaged that bonuses would be paid where profits are significant.

Included in this forecast is the capital expenditure mentioned earlier (£100,000) plus additional expenditure as shown below:

Potential Replacement Equipment

ICP (November 2001)	£60,000
GC (February 2002)	£30,000
HPLC (April 2002)	£30,000

Capacity Improvement Equipment

Discrete Analyser (August 2001)	£100,000
EZ Flash (August 2001)	In total
Large capacity HPLC auto sampler (August 2001)	
Organics liquid/liquid extraction system (Oct 2001)	£35,000

A more detailed breakdown of the non-growth and continued growth forecasts is provided below:

	Non-Growth	Continued Growth
Turnover	4,273,226	5,594,464
Payroll costs	1,821,408	1,956,897
Materials and consumables costs	676,970	895,383
Transport costs	147,187	201,702
Other operating costs	566,762	467,524
Depreciation	231,132	248,083
Total costs	3,443,459	3,769,589
Operating profit	829,766	1,824,875

Note: These figures are shown before any adjustment to arrive at maintainable earnings.

7. Arrangements for Offers

Deadline for offers and where to submit them

This document will be provided only to those parties who have expressed a strong interest in purchasing the company and have signed a confidentiality agreement. They have already visited the company and had initial discussions with the managing director and chairman.

Upon receipt of this document interested parties should make in writing a written indicative offer. The company will respond to all offers. If the company should decide to accept an offer Heads of Agreement will be drawn up. Once this has been completed due diligence may commence.

Arrangements for visits and negotiations (on or off site announcements)

This document is intended to provide sufficient information for a prospective buyer to make an indicative offer to purchase the company. Whilst it is recognised that additional information or clarification may be required, at this stage there will be no further opportunity to provide this. All contact with the company will be conducted only through the managing director (Steve xxxxxx) or in his absence the finance director (xxxxxx). Attached as an appendix (appendix 3) are specific requests for information that the company has received from an interested purchaser.

8. Caveats

To the best of the knowledge and belief of the directors the information contained in this document is accurate. This is not a public offer document. The information contained within this document is for the private use of the reader.

10 *From offer to payment*

On the last lap

The ideal situation is that you have more than one buyer interested in your business – you can't beat a bit of competition for driving up the asking price. Even if you only have one buyer, try to create a bit of mystery, just to let the one serious buyer think they are under some pressure to come up with a better offer.

Case study

A good friend of mine, Jerry, had a lovely business but one part of it (electronic component wholesaling) was really struggling, especially post-11 September. It was a significant business (turnover around £2 million) but it was barely profitable and to be honest not really where his interest lay. He spoke to me about selling it and we scratched our heads about who would buy it and at what price. At the time it appeared that the best offers were from other smaller, similar businesses trying to consolidate to stay in business – buy in the turnover, strip out the costs and improve the combined bottom line. The interest and offers were derisory; very little cash was involved, in fact one tentative offer was really a share swap. I suggested to Jerry that he stopped talking to everyone and concentrated on a few months of grooming the business. He got on with this and told the interested parties that all bets were off.

Six months later the business was marginally better, but the economic climate had changed. He had had another approach but, feeling more confident, Jerry was inclined to be more bullish. The buyer made a verbal offer of £1 million – far better than the offers six months before. Jerry's response was quite cool (so I thought). He told them the deal he wanted. First, he wanted pound for pound for turnover, which meant £2 million. Second, he wanted £1 million up front and the rest over two years against agreed financial results. Finally, he told them that he already had an offer at this level and that he needed a written offer within seven days or he would sell to the other buyer (obviously a competitor of theirs). Wow, talk about piling on the pressure! Jerry knew that they had a board meeting that week and he also knew that he could force the issue high up their agenda that day by taking this approach. Sure enough, the board agreed the deal: a revised offer was forthcoming. They asked Jerry to stop negotiations with the other buyer (fictitious of course) – they wanted exclusivity. Jerry phoned me just before Easter 2002 to ask me if I knew a good lawyer to get the rest of the deal (payment and tax planning) done. It looks like the apparent competition has brought Jerry a better deal than he would otherwise have got. Well done, I say.

Of course Jerry is not home and dry yet – at this stage all he has is a written offer of intent. This is not a binding contract: there are enough holes in it for either party to escape through. However, it is the start of the final lap and it is worthwhile seeing what it could look like – just so you are forearmed.

Handling enquiries/offers

The last thing you want is for the cat to slip out of the bag. The period during which 'suits' are visiting your company to find out enough to make an offer and then carry out due diligence can be several weeks. During this time you need to have set procedures in place to minimise the risk of your staff finding out that the company is for sale.

Confidentiality

There are a number of basic procedures that can be set down to try and maintain confidentiality:

- Make sure that as few people as possible within the company know about the sale process and that they are fully aware of the need for confidentiality.
- Make sure outside advisers are similarly briefed.

- Make sure you have a 'cover story' to account for all the increased activity, eg they are here to carry out the preliminary work for a flotation; this always goes down well and provides good cover for accountants, lawyers, etc.

- Ensure all visitors to the business are discreet and stick to the agreed 'cover story'.

- Restrict all calls, e-mails, faxes and mail to the business.

- Make sure that a suitable confidentiality letter has been signed before sensitive information is made available.

- Keep all direct contact between the sellers and interested parties to a minimum.

- Make sure you have a fall-back position in case the story gets out. Have pre-arranged explanations for suppliers, customers, staff, etc. My view is that you should think very carefully about what you tell your staff and when.

Handling enquiries

In most cases a seller will use an intermediary. This will mean that many of the meetings and all correspondence can safely be kept 'off site'. A senior director should be nominated as the only point of contact for all external enquiries/sending out of information. If you are doing it yourself then you will need to give buyers a special phone number and box number for correspondence. As an alternative you could insist that all contact be via the senior director's home phone/address, though this can be quite restrictive.

Datarooms

Quite often the information memorandum will not contain sufficient information, especially in the case of a large and complex company. A common way of making information available to buyers to finalise their offers is the use of a dataroom. Basically all the relevant financial records and information that are considered necessary are made available in one room and interested parties are allowed to spend an agreed period of time reviewing the information before making their offer.

Handling offers

The process can either be informal of formal – it really depends on your style. The informal approach can be to allow interested parties to visit the company, meet the owners and ask questions on the information memorandum before making an offer. Alternatively, meetings can be held 'off site' to avoid arousing suspicion among staff, and buyers are only permitted to visit the company before finalising their offers. This approach may be better if there are likely to be several bidders for the company. At some stage the buyer will need to see the company and if it can be arranged it is best to get them in early on. This will leave fewer unanswered questions and will lead to better-quality offers.

Typical offer letter

The following offer letter is fairly typical of what you might receive if you were selling your business. I have tried to remove most of the 'legalise' to make it more understandable to the non-legal mind. The letter does not need to be long – two pages will normally suffice. Its purpose is to signify the serious intent of the buyer, the price they are prepared to pay and how it will be paid. It lays down the rules regarding confidentiality, the timescales involved, the necessity of exclusivity and the financial threat if you do not proceed in good faith.

PRIVATE AND CONFIDENTIAL – FOR ADDRESEE ONLY

Beechwood Enterprises
Pear Tree Cottage
South Cerney
Glos GL7 5US

SUBJECT TO CONTRACT

Date: 02 April 2004

To: Directors/majority shareholders
Target Company Limited

Dear Sirs

Target Company Limited

We are writing to set out the main terms and conditions under which we are prepared to purchase all the issued share capital of the Company (Transaction). Apart from paragraphs ix and x none of the terms and conditions of this letter is intended to be binding. However, this letter may form the basis of a legally binding agreement at a later date. Paragraphs ix and x, which refer to confidentiality, lock out period and costs shall become legally binding as soon as you countersign this letter.

i. Shares to be acquired
All the issued share capital of Target Company Limited (Shares).

ii. Price
The maximum price payable by us for the Shares will be £3 million, which will be paid as £2 million in cash upon completion and £1 million of loan stock.

iii. Conditions
This Transaction will be conditional on our satisfaction with due diligence.

iv. Representations, warranties and indemnities
The agreement to acquire the Shares will contain any representations, warranties and indemnities that we consider necessary and appropriate.

v. Completion
Completion of this Transaction will take place on or before 03 May 2004.

vi. Service agreements
xxxxxxxxxx (MD) and xxxxxxxxxx (Operations Director) will enter into two-year service agreements with the Company prior to the Transaction.

vii. Auditors
The current auditors of the Company will resign as from the date of completion.

viii. Commercial restrictions
The sellers will give an undertaking not to compete in the same area of business for two years after completion. In addition they will give an undertaking not to solicit or procure any staff, suppliers and customers from the company either on their own behalf or for another principal.

ix. Enforceable undertakings
All parties agree to treat as strictly confidential any information revealed to them during the course of negotiations and to be liable for any loss or damage that may arise out of the unauthorised disclosure of any such information.

All parties also agree that no announcements regarding these negotiations or the Transaction will be made by any of the parties without the prior written consent of the others.

Before we proceed to due diligence and incur any expenses in terms of management time and advisers' fees and in consideration of our agreeing to the confidentiality provisions set out above you will agree to the following:

1. to cease any discussions with any other party regarding the disposal of the Shares or any other material assets of the Company, and
2. not to enter into any discussions with any other party regarding the disposal of the Shares or any other material assets of the Company until 02 May 2004, and
3. use your best efforts to negotiate an agreement for the sale and purchase of Shares as outlined in this letter, and
4. use your best efforts to ensure that during this period of negotiation the business is run in a proper manner that is consistent with good commercial practice.

Paragraphs ix and x will become legally enforceable immediately upon countersignature of this letter.

x. Costs
All parties undertake with the others that they will bear their own costs and pay their own expenses in relation to the Transaction.

You will pay our reasonable costs and expenses if you are in breach of paragraph ix or otherwise fail to deal in good faith with us. Our reasonable costs and expenses will include those incurred by our professional advisers and financiers.

When you have read and fully understood the full contents of this letter will you please confirm your acceptance of the above terms and conditions by signing and returning to us the attached copy of this letter no later than 08 April 2004.

Yours sincerely

_____

For and on behalf of Beechwood Enterprises

We confirm our agreement to the full terms and conditions set out in this letter.

_____

Signature

_____

Signature

Date: ——————————————

I don't think I need to say any more on the offer letter. If you accept then just sign and return it. Obviously, if there is anything you violently disagree with then take legal advice before responding, otherwise it's on to negotiating the deal.

Negotiating the deal

Obviously the offer letter is not the final deal – it is the opening salvo. It needs to be expanded into the detailed deal structure. The process will eventually lead to 'heads of agreement' and then a sale and purchase contract. Let's look at the events leading up to the signing of heads of agreement.

Expectations

Obviously the owners of the business have been told the likely selling price by their advisers. It is sometimes possible that they get an inflated view based on hearsay (talking to ill-informed friends or associates), or ill-informed advisers (who are not in touch with the market), or expecting a capital sum that will provide the same income that they used to receive from the business (ignoring the fact that once sold they run no risk and cannot therefore expect the same level of return). They should not ignore the facts that dictate the guide price, which are: previous deals; financial strength of the company; and cash now or cash tomorrow (you may achieve a higher price if you accept a deferred consideration over, say, two or three years). Another consideration will be the owners' taxation position – this will have a major influence on how much of the sale proceeds they will eventually end up with. Finally, both the owners and the advisers must know the realistic price and the bottom line figure that they will accept – the f*** off price as one of my friends used to call it, ie the price that they would require to f*** off and leave the company behind.

Carrying out the negotiations

There is great merit in letting a third party carry out the negotiations: it separates the sellers and the buyers and stops it from getting personal. A professional negotiator will be able to fend off unrealistic offers, conditions of purchase, deferred payment schemes, etc as a matter of course without upsetting the seller. Certainly where the buyer is a listed plc using its considerable muscle to acquire a considerably smaller owner-managed company, using a professional negotiator will start to even things up a little. If the sellers are using a professional negotiator then the parameters must be agreed in advance. All meetings should be planned carefully and all parties from the company should be well prepared. A worthwhile tactic to influence the negotiations is to feed in good news to the purchaser at an appropriate time, such as a big new order coming in, or a competitor going bust.

What are they buying – share or assets?

From a seller's point of view it is usually more advantageous to sell shares – there are taxation advantages in using this route (covered later). From a buyer's point of view there may be a preference to acquire specified assets and take on agreed liabilities, which reduces their risk as all other liabilities not listed are excluded. Neither option removes the company's responsibilities to its employees (TUPE – see Chapter 8).

Heads of agreement

This is really more appropriate if a verbal offer has been made, supported by correspondence. It signifies the moving to the pre-completion or nitty-gritty stage, where the fine detail of the deal is agreed and committed to paper. However, if an offer letter exists, quite frequently the heads of agreement stage is bypassed and all parties progress straight to due diligence. Usually the heads of agreement will contain what we have seen in the offer letter plus things like any pre-sale conditions, such as restrictions on dividends, cash strip, and due diligence requirements.

Due diligence

A buyer uses due diligence to find out about the company that is being bought. During the investigation (usually carried out by independent accountants) financial and other company records will be examined to establish how sound the company is. This will cover areas such as financial records, supplier contracts, customer contracts, employment contracts, patents, trademarks, product/services, management structure and outstanding legal matters. It is like a very thorough audit performed over a short period of time, designed to find any 'skeletons in the cupboard'. If anything nasty turns up during this process the buyer will either walk away or use it to renegotiate the price – downwards.

The financial backer of the buyer is also interested in the due diligence process: it will determine whether the financial support will be available. Also, it is not uncommon for the buyer to impose additional warranties and indemnities on the seller if they were unhappy with certain aspects of the business as a result of due diligence. In addition the buyer may insist on a large element of deferred consideration (payment later) to give them added comfort if they are unsure about certain aspects of the business as a result of due diligence.

We covered due diligence briefly in Chapter 7 on grooming your business for sale. Take my tip and carry out your own due diligence – 'vendor due diligence' as it is called. It is easier to manage and can pre-empt those major issues that can wreck a deal. It also ensures that the time between heads of agreement/offer letter and completion is reduced.

Sale and purchase contract

This is the main document, which sets out in some detail the terms of the deal. It can be quite lengthy, especially in the case of an asset purchase, because it will have to detail every asset (and liability) being taken on by the buyer. In a share purchase the only thing being transferred is the company shares, so the document is simpler. However, because there is greater business risk in buying shares there are likely to be considerable warranties and indemnities. A warranty is an assurance that a particular state of affairs is correct. If this is not true the person giving the warranty (the seller) is liable to pay compensation to the buyer for any loss suffered. An indemnity is where the seller undertakes to make good the liability if a particular event (or set of events) occurs. A typical area for indemnities is taxation, where the seller agrees to indemnify the buyers for any subsequent tax claims as a result of events prior to the purchase.

It is not uncommon for the seller to seek to limit liability under these headings in the sale and purchase contract by setting *de minimis* limits to avoid small claims. For example, the contract may state that no claims below £1,000 can be made and that in total they cannot exceed £50,000. The seller will also seek to disclose all potential liabilities in an attempt to limit any further claim for damages by the purchaser. It is possible to take out insurance cover against warranty claims.

It is outside the scope of this book to show a typical sale and purchase contract (the buyer's lawyers will prepare this) but typically it will cover:

- definitions and interpretation;
- type of sale – asset/share;
- consideration – how much, when, and in what form (cash, shares, loan notes, etc);
- completion – when;
- escrow account – arrangements for retention of some of the sale proceeds to cover warranties, etc;
- completion accounts – statement showing where all the sale proceeds went (lawyers, accountants, etc);

- obligations of the parties;
- restrictions on sellers;
- warranties;
- tax covenants;
- announcements;
- confidentiality;
- costs;
- other;
- governing law;
- numerous schedules covering shares being transferred, group structure, property, warranties, etc.

When the legal wrangling is over and this is signed by all parties (buyer and seller) and exchanged, then the deal is done – no backing out. On completion day the funds will be transferred and the company has a new owner. However, before that time I would just like to point out two other areas of concern to anyone selling their business – deal structures and taxation.

Deal structures

There is a whole range of possibilities when it comes to payment: cash (some today and some tomorrow), loan notes and share swaps are typical. Obviously taxation will be a consideration (nobody likes paying too much tax) but don't let undue attempts to avoid tax spoil a good commercial deal. Be very wary of entering into complex deal structures purely for tax purposes. These arrangements frequently involve deferred consideration (over several tax years) and if the buyer is not financially sound the seller runs the risk of not getting paid. Let's look briefly at the options:

- Cash on completion – obviously the preferred option to the seller. Payable by bankers draft into the seller's bank account, it gives certainty but may not always be the most tax-efficient (see taxation, below).

- Cash plus an element of deferred payment – the following options are used and are listed in what I would regard as their order of preference (from a seller's point of view):

  - loan notes backed by a UK bank guarantee – rock solid;

  - loan notes backed by buyer's guarantee or security (eg charge over company assets) – not so solid and dependent on the financial strength of the buyer;

  - loan notes with no security – risky (don't touch with a barge pole);

  - 'earn out', which is basically additional future consideration based on the financial performance of the company just sold – very risky as the seller can have little or no influence over this and the buyer can (through questionable accounting) reduce the profits thereby reducing or eliminating altogether any future consideration;

  - retaining an equity stake in the business sold (with an option for the buyer to acquire these later) – don't ignore this option as it can prove attractive if the seller believes that the business will do even better in the hands of the buyer. It offers a 'second bite at the cherry';

  - shares (paper) in the purchaser – don't touch it if the company is not quoted. This will be the preferred option for most large quoted trade buyers. If you accept any consideration in this way, remember that shares can go down as well as up and that you can often end up with less than you had planned. Always ask yourself the question, 'Would I of my own free will invest such a large sum of money in this company?'

- All-deferred consideration – highly risky. Better jam today than jam tomorrow. Only suitable if there is a large tax liability that can be avoided by taking this approach.

Obviously all these options are part of the negotiations. I always tell my clients that they should be happy with the cash they get on completion and treat any deferred consideration as a bonus (because they may not get it).

Pre-sale payments can be relevant. Should you clear out all the cash from your company prior to sale? Should you pay yourself big dividends and bonuses? And what about some hefty pension contributions? If yours is an owner-managed business you have a right to do this. If you decide on this option, do it long before you start negotiations with a buyer as it often complicates matters. Also, remember that if you take out £100,000 in dividends you are likely to pay tax at 40 per cent. If you leave it in the company when you sell it and can persuade the buyer to pay full (or near full) value for it you may only pay tax at 10 per cent on it – I leave the decision to you.

Taxation

Considering the tax implications of selling a business would warrant a book in itself. The simple message I always give my clients is: take tax advice. If you sell a business any profit you make will be subject to capital gains tax (CGT). Fortunately, successive governments have smiled favourably on owner-managers cashing in (sorry, selling their business). However, there is no certainty that this will last. Here are the basics of CGT, as guidance only: do check out your particular circumstances with an expert.

Calculating the gain – broadly the capital gain is calculated on the difference between proceeds realised and the historic cost of the asset being sold. Apparently the Inland Revenue doesn't have much to say on what proceeds are taken into account, but in practice it means all cash (at completion, deferred, earn outs, pre-sale dividends) plus shares received (at valuation) plus any other assets received (cars, boats, etc).

Calculating any reliefs available to reduce the capital gain – basically there are two type of relief available, taper relief or retirement relief (which was fully phased out during tax year 2002/2003). Since by the time this book is published retirement relief will be all but over, I will only mention taper relief.

Taper relief

There are two factors that determine how much taper relief is available: where the assets being sold (this includes shares) are classified as business assets (according to Inland Revenue rules) through the 'relevant period of ownership', and the length of time these assets have been held since the date of acquisition.

Business assets can be any of the following:

- shares in a 'qualifying company' owned by the seller;

- assets used for the purposes of a trade carried on by the seller;

- an asset used for the purposes of a trade carried on by the seller's qualifying company;

- any asset the seller held as a requirement of their employment to which they were required to devote 'substantially the whole of their time'.

A qualifying company must be either a trading company or the holding company of a trading group. Prior to 5 April 2000 the conditions on shareholdings qualifying as business assets were more severe, but this has been relaxed as from 6 April 2000:

6 April 1998 to 5 April 2000:
– trading company with 25 per cent of voting rights, or
– trading company with 5 per cent of voting rights and full time employee.

From 6 April 2000 onwards:
– unquoted trading company, or
– seller is an officer or employee, or
– seller has 5 per cent of voting rights of listed company.

Any assets which, throughout the period of ownership, have been used both as a business asset and as a non-qualifying business asset will have the gain on their disposal apportioned pro-rata. However, the Inland Revenue tends to ignore non-business assets that are not substantial (less than 20 per cent of total assets sold).

The taper relief available then depends on how many complete years the asset has been held since 5 April 1998. The longer the seller has held the asset the greater the relief available and the lower the CGT payable. Fortunately, we can thank the current Labour government for greatly simplifying and reducing the tax burden on owners selling their business assets (that includes shares). In effect, after just two years of ownership of business assets the capital gain is reduced by 75 per cent (the maximum) but non-business assets will take 10 years to be reduced by 40 per cent (the maximum).

Table 10.1 shows the effective rate of tax paid on capital gains split between the rates chargeable for business assets and non-business assets.

Table 10.1   The effective rate of tax paid on capital gains

| | **% of chargeable gain** | |
Number of years in qualifying ownership	**Business asset**	**Non-business asset**
1	50	100
2	25	100
3	25	95
4	25	90
5	25	85
6	25	80
7	25	75
8	25	70
9	25	65
10+	25	60

I think the simple message is that the split between business and non-business assets is critical – this may take some planning, but the tax benefits are obvious. In practice it means that if you sell a business that you have owned for just two years and all the assets are deemed to be business assets you will end up paying an effective tax rate of 10 per cent as a higher rate tax payer (40 per cent tax rate x 25 per cent gain). By any standards this is a good deal.

Rollover relief and the Enterprise Investment Scheme (EIS)

There are two other reliefs that I will mention in passing which may help to shelter some of the gain from CGT.

Rollover relief – this cannot be used to shelter gains from share sales but can be used to shelter gains from asset sales such as land, buildings, fixed plant and machinery, goodwill, etc. The relief is available to the extent that any proceeds received from the sale of these qualifying assets are used to purchase another asset for use wholly for business purposes in the same or another trade. Basically, if you make a gain out of selling a qualifying business asset you can postpone the gain (rollover) by investing it in another business asset. This may be useful if the taper relief does not shelter sufficient gains from tax.

EIS – if an individual has made an investment in a qualifying company under this scheme any gain from it will (subject to some Inland Revenue rules) be free from CGT. A maximum of £150,000 in each tax year can be invested in new shares, for which the investor will receive 20 per cent tax relief. You can see how EIS could be used in conjunction with rollover relief to shelter further capital gains from tax that could not be avoided under taper relief or retirement relief.

Going abroad

I suppose I ought to briefly mention the age-old option of going abroad to avoid paying CGT. It is still an option, but with world harmonisation of taxes (especially in Europe) it is less practical: some other countries have higher CGT regimes than the UK and you would, by being resident there, be liable to the local tax system. However, if the country you choose does not have a worse tax regime then it might be worth considering, but remember, since 1998 it has become necessary to go abroad for longer: think seriously about this option and the disruption to you partner, children, and other family. How would they (and you) cope if you had to go and live in Belgium (sorry Belgium), learn a new language and be part of a different culture? Also, if such a move is not planned well in advance of the sale, the Inland Revenue will still catch you out, so don't leave it to the last minute.

As I have already mentioned, I cannot provide anything other than scant coverage to the tax aspects of selling your business. However, I hope this gives you some initial guidance – *but do speak to a tax expert before you sell your business.*

What about your last lap?

Have you got your team of expert advisers lined up and on your side? Do they know what your personal financial objectives are? Brief them properly to do what you want, not what is easiest for them. I should warn you that the last lap can be quite tough, but the rewards will be worth it.

Let me remind you of how my friend Jim feels with £4 million in the bank after he had cashed in – free to do what he wants to do. Good luck and enjoy the rest of your life. And if you are feeling generous and want to give me a bit too – thank you, but tell a friend how I helped and maybe I can help them as well.

Chapter summary

In this chapter we have looked at getting from offer to payment. It can be quite complex and will require the help of both lawyers and accountants to get it right. On the last lap, don't undo all the good work you have done in grooming and marketing your business for sale. If you want paying in cash now, don't be talked into a deferred payment arrangement. Also, work out in advance (before you agree the deal structure) how much cash you will end up with after tax. This may influence how you structure the deal.

Finally, although I have only mentioned it briefly, do think about the rest of your life – how you want to live it, where you want to live it. For goodness sake, is it worth saving a small amount of tax for a lifetime of misery?

Sources of help

This is not a textbook and as such it does not contain the fullest depth of information you may possibly need to do everything mentioned. The following sources of help are all known to me and are among those that I have used in the past. At the time of writing (January 2004) the information is correct to the best of my knowledge and the Web sites working. The basic information shown below has come from the Web sites of each organisation listed. If no telephone number is shown it is only because they have not provided a central number.

General help

The British Chambers of Commerce
Tel: 020 7654 5800
Web site: http://www.britishchambers.org.uk

Business Link Helpline (to find out your nearest Business Link)
Tel: 0845 600 9 006
Web site: http://www.businesslink.gov.uk/bdotg/action/home

Companies Registration Office
Tel: 0870 33 33 636
Web site: http://www.companieshouse.gov.uk

Cranfield University
Web site: http://www.som.cranfield.ac.uk/som/

Like most good universities, Cranfield offers a range of programmes for owner-managed businesses. It specifically runs programmes for owners wanting to grow and sell their businesses. I suggest that you look at the School of Management site.

HM Customs and Excise
Tel: 0845 010 9000
Web site: http://www.hmce.gov.uk

Board of Inland Revenue
Web site: http://www.inlandrevenue.gov.uk (includes listing of telephone numbers)

Institute of Directors
Tel:020 7766 8866
Web site: http://www.iod.com/

Patents Office and Trade Marks
Tel:08459 500 505
Web site: http://www.patent.gov.uk/

Department of Trade and Industry
Tel: 01207 215 5000
Web site: http://www.dti.gov.uk/

Finance

Alternative Investment Market (AIM)
Web site: http://www.londonstockexchange.com/aim/default.asp

Association of British Insurers
Tel: 020 7600 3333
Web site: http://www.abi.org.uk

British Bankers Association
Web site: http://www.bba.org.uk

BVCA
British Venture Capital Association
Tel: 020 7025 2950
Web site: http://www.bvca.co.uk

Business Angel network
Obviously there is no direct way of contacting Business Angels, but most Business Links have access to their own local network. Another way to contact them is to get in touch with the BVCA and ask for their publication, *Sources of Business Angel Capital*. Below are some useful links to tap into the Business Angel network.

The Venture Site
Not-for-profit UK matchmaking for Business Angels and entrepreneurs since 1997. The site looks a bit amateurish but Barclays sponsors it.
Web site: http://www.venturesite.co.uk

Bestmatch
National Business Angels Network, the biggest portal to the UK informal investment market. You can use Bestmatch to locate and choose an adviser to help you find your way through the Business Angel market, or if you wish you can phone, on 020 7246 0765 for further assistance. It will be replaced in due course by Angelgateway and NBANexchange, but at the time of writing these are not up and running.
Web site: http://www.nationalbusangels.co.uk

Business money
Tel: 01458 253536
For up-to-date information on current commercial rates. It also includes a commercial mortgage calculator.
Web site: http://www.business-money.com

DTI Loan Guarantee Scheme
Tel: 0845 001 0032/0033
Web site: http://www.dti.gov.uk/sflg

Factors and Discounters Association
Tel: 020 8332 9955
Web site: http://www.factors.org.uk

Finance and Leasing Association
Tel: 020 7836 6511
Web site: http://www.fla.org.uk

London Stock Exchange (Full listing)
Web site: http://www.londonstockexchange.com/

Finding professional advisers

Institute of Chartered Accountants in England and Wales
Tel: 020 7324 2351
Web site: http://www.icaewfirms.co.uk/ (directory of local firms)

Institute of Chartered Accountants in Scotland
Web site: http://www.icas.org.uk/directory/index.asp (directory of local
firms)

Institute of Chartered Accountants in Northern Ireland
Tel: 353 1 637 7200 (Dublin) and 028 9032 1600 (Belfast)
Web site: http://www.chartered-accountants.co.uk – covers all the account-
ing institutes in the UK.

Law Society
Tel: 0207 242 1222
Web site: http://www.lawsociety.org.uk/

Sites specifically for buying and selling businesses

Grant Thornton
Web site: http://www.companiesforsale.uk.com

Daltons (the same people that print the weekly paper)
Web site: http://www.daltonsbusiness.com/Companiesforsale.asp

The Business Sale Report
Web site: www.business-sale.com

Useful publications

Oxford Dictionary of Finance and Banking, edited by Brian Butler, David
    Butler and Alan Isaacs, Oxford University Press, ISBN: 0 192 80067 1
Corporate Finance Handbook, Consultant Editor: Jonathan Reuvid, Kogan
    Page/KPMG, ISBN: 0 749 43626 3
The Bottom Line, Paul Barrow, Virgin Books, ISBN: 0 753 5056 9

How to contact Paul Barrow

Please contact me by e-mail at paul@pauljamesbarrow.freeserve.co.uk

Glossary

I apologise if I have used some words or expressions in this book that you may not be familiar with. Hopefully this glossary, which I believe to be comprehensive, should cover all the specialist terms in the book that would be outside the normal knowledge of a businessperson.

Alternative Investment Market (AIM)   AIM replaced the Unlisted Securities Market (USM) in June 1995 as the secondary market of the London Stock Exchange for small, growing companies to raise capital and have their shares traded. It is a lower cost, less formal route than a full market listing. There has been some criticism of AIM in that share prices and movement are controlled by market makers/company stockbrokers and as such a free market does not always exist.

asset-based finance   Asset-based finance allows funding to be secured against business assets such as debtors, stock, machinery and property. Typically a business can borrow around 85 per cent of outstanding debtors, 30–50 per cent of work in progress, 80 per cent of plant and machinery. The real benefit of this type of facility is that as you stock up and sell, more cash becomes available. The two main types of asset-based finance used are factoring and invoice discounting (*see* below).

balance sheet audit   A balance sheet audit will systematically construct and verify the balance sheet for the business you are buying. This will be done from the records that the business has. In addition, your accountant will seek third-party verification of the figures, eg debtor, creditor and bank balance confirmation.

bank loan (Also known as a 'term loan'.) A more formal arrangement than a bank overdraft (*see* below) whereby a set amount is borrowed and repayment of capital and interest are made by monthly (or quarterly) repayments over the term of the loan. The interest rate is usually fixed for the period of the loan and once granted the loan cannot usually be withdrawn before the end of the agreed loan period. Interest is calculated for the full period of the loan and added to the capital to calculate the repayments. Quite often there can be penalty payments for early repayment of a loan.

bank overdraft The traditional British business solution to term and long-term financing. An overdraft is a loan made by a bank to an individual or company for short-term purposes. A maximum limit is agreed (overdraft limit) and the loan is made available for an agreed period, typically up to 12 months. It is usually possible to renew this facility and a renewal fee is usually charged. Interest is charged on a daily basis (and may vary according to the prevailing bank rate) and what really sets it apart from a traditional bank loan is that no fixed repayment schedule is set up. The bank will either call in the loan in full, which it can do at any time, or the individual or business repays the overdraft as and when funds become available.

broker or stockbroker A securities firm that provides advice and dealing services to the public and which can deal on its own account. Some brokers on AIM act as market makers, which means they effectively set the price and control all buying and selling of shares in their registered companies.

Business Angels Usually high-worth individuals who make equity (shares purchase) investments in businesses. Quite frequently, as well as money they can bring valuable skills and contacts to a business. They will typically commit amounts of between £10,000 and £100,000 to a single business. Unfortunately Business Angels want to remain anonymous so you will not find them in *Yellow Pages* – this stops them being swamped with proposals.

buy-in management buy-out (BIMBO) A combination of a management buy out and a management buy in.

confidentiality agreement   During commercial negotiations it is vital that you protect any commercial data belonging to you or your organisation. This legal agreement will protect that information and ensure it is dealt with in a professional manner.

Key clauses in this agreement include: protection against the copying or retention of confidential information; protection against disclosure of information not already in the public domain; and remedy for any breach of the agreement. Sometimes a confidentiality agreement is referred to as a 'non-disclosure agreement' (NDA).

contract hire   Essentially the same as leasing (see below) but commonly used for motor vehicles where the service, maintenance and road fund licence costs can be included in the monthly charge to provide a business with predictable costs. The contract hire will be, in this example, for an agreed total mileage with an additional charge being made for excess mileage.

dataroom   A common way of making information available to buyers to finalise their offers. Basically, all the relevant financial records and other commercially sensitive information that are considered necessary are made available in one room where interested parties are allowed to spend an agreed period of time reviewing the information before making their offer. They may not take copies of the information but they may make notes.

dividend strip   A perfectly legitimate process for removing excess cash in a business prior to a sale by means of declaring additional dividends. Generally not a very tax-efficient way of removing value, but if the buyer will not give you full value for the excess cash or the Inland Revenue has deemed it to be a non-business asset, then it may be worthwhile.

due diligence   This is the process by which the buyer tries to ensure that what they are buying is what they see. It will flush out any inherent weaknesses in the business, eg management team, financial issues and customers. If anything is not in order it will be identified and used by the buyer to negotiate the price downwards. Smart sellers do their own due diligence first (known as 'vendor due diligence'), which picks up any problems before the buyer gets to see it. However, it is important to get vendor due diligence done by a top rate firm of chartered accountants who are not your auditors.

earn out   Sometimes a buyer will agree to pay an incentive (an 'earn out') to the owner to encourage them to remain in the business and thereby avoid bearing the entire risk of the acquisition. In return for being tied in to the business the former owner receives a share of profits earned over a two or three-year period. *A word of caution:* in most cases the buyer seeks to avoid paying the earn out, by fair means or foul. This is the experience of many sellers, so get as much cash up front as possible.

Employee Share Ownership Plan (Esop)   This is a plan that allows employees to participate in their businesses on a significant scale in a tax-efficient way. Shares acquired under an Inland Revenue-approved Esop scheme enjoy almost total exemption from income tax and capital gains tax provided the shares are held long enough.

Enterprise Investment Scheme (EIS)   The EIS is a government intro-duced scheme that allows certain tax reliefs for investors who invest in qualifying shares in qualifying companies. In summary, an investment up to £150,000 per annum in ordinary shares will give the investor 20 per cent of this sum as tax relief. In addition, if the asset is disposed of after three years there will be no capital gains tax (CGT) due. There is provision for CGT deferral if the asset is sold before this time.

equity funding   The appropriate source of long-term finance for high-risk business projects where little or no security is available. The business issues and sells new shares (equity) in exchange for the cash injected. Banks do not offer this service but venture capitalists, Business Angels, IPOs or flotations are all ways of raising equity funding.

factoring   Using this the business 'sells' its invoices to a factor (usually part of a bank) and contracts its sales ledger administration to the factor. The customer knows the facility is in place because it is paying a factor instead of its supplier. Factoring used to have a stigma attached to it in the early years – the assumption was if you were factoring you were short of cash and going bust. Factoring can include full bad debt protection (called non-recourse factoring) or exclude bad debt cover (recourse factoring). The former is more expensive because it covers an element of bad debt insurance, so that the factor cannot have any comeback (recourse) against the business if the debt goes bad. Usually available for businesses achieving or forecasting turnover of around £50,000 plus per annum.

grooming   Owners are able to significantly improve the price achieved upon sale by careful planning. It is never too early for a business owner or owners to start to plan for the eventual route out of, or succession to, the business. Grooming is the process of preparing or positioning a business for sale to improve its attractiveness and value to potential buyers. This process may take between six months and two years and will include such activities as profit improvement, vendor due diligence, etc.

heads of agreement   This is really only appropriate if a verbal offer has been made, supported by correspondence. It signifies the moving to the pre-completion stage, where the fine detail of the deal is agreed and committed to paper. Usually the heads of agreement will contain what was in the offer letter plus things like any pre-sale conditions, eg restrictions on dividends, cash strip and due diligence requirements.

hire purchase (HP)   Similar to a bank loan in operation (*see* above) whereby assets are purchased by means of a loan. Ownership of the asset remains with the finance company until the final payment has been made, but the purchaser enjoys possession immediately. In most HP agreements a deposit (quite often the equivalent of about three months' payments) is paid up front.

information memorandum   A document prepared by a business (usually their advisers) that is up for sale and circulated to prospective buyers. Its purpose is to show the business in its most positive light to attract the highest selling price. While the directors are responsible for the accuracy of this document, 'weasel' words are included to try and avoid any liability as a result of a buyer using this information for the purpose of buying the company. It is in effect a mini business plan aimed at selling the business.

initial public offering (IPO)   An American term for a share flotation, although this term is now being used in the UK. The process of launching a public company for the first time and inviting members of the public to subscribe for shares. In the UK the term 'going public' has the same meaning.

institutional buy-out (IBO)   The purchase of a company by a private equity firm following which the incumbent and/or incoming management will be given or acquire a stake in the business. This has some similarities to MBO and MBI (*see* below).

invoice discounting   (Also known as confidential discounting.) Using this the business exchanges sales invoices for cash but retains full control over its own invoicing and debtor collection. The customer does not know the facility is in place – they pay the supplier as normal. Avoids the 'stigma' of factoring. Bad debt protection can be provided as part of this package, but invoice discounting will usually be a cheaper form of debtor financing if no other service is being used. Usually available for businesses achieving or forecasting turnover of around £750,000 plus (with no upper limit).

leasing   Under a leasing agreement you pay (usually monthly) to use an asset for an agreed period of time. At the end of the agreed period (term) you return the asset (in good condition) to its owner – you do not ever acquire ownership of the asset. Also referred to as 'off balance sheet financing' because neither the asset nor the liability for the financing appears on the balance sheet.

leveraged build-up (LBU)   When a private equity firm buys a company as principal with the aim of making further relevant acquisitions to develop an enlarged business group.

leveraged buy-out (LBO)   The purchase of a controlling proportion of the shares of a company by its own management, financed almost exclusively by borrowing. This leads to the further terms 'highly geared' or 'highly leveraged', which describe the risky financing of these businesses, especially in recessionary/highly competitive economic climates.

loan notes   A legally binding promise, by means of a document (loan note) by which the debtor offers to repay the agreed sum due on a fixed date in the future. Interest is due on the outstanding amount and provision will be made in the loan note for this. The strength of the loan note lies in the strength of the party issuing it. You can rely on a loan note guaranteed by a UK bank, but would you want one from a privately owned business?

management buy-in (MBI)   Where an external manager or group of managers uses external funding to buy into or acquire a business from the owners. Funded in the same way as an MBO.

management buy-out (MBO)   Where the existing management buy the business from the owners using funds provided by banks (loans) and typically a private equity house (equity funding and mezzanine debt).

mezzanine debt   Debt that incorporates some equity-based benefits and rights. Mezzanine debt is actually closer to equity than debt, in that the debt is usually only of importance in the event of bankruptcy. Mezzanine debt is often used to finance acquisitions and buy outs, where it can be used to prioritise new owners ahead of existing owners in the event that a bankruptcy occurs. It is unsecured and ranks behind senior (or secured) debt – hence the element of risk and reward.

NewCo   A new limited company set up specifically for a buyer to acquire an existing business, with the main purpose of ensuring that the 'muddy' or uncertain past of the business being acquired is lost, eg outstanding corporation tax and NI/PAYE problems and creditor claims. The NewCo has a clean start, just taking over what it wants, eg the customers, trade marks, patents, right to business and selected assets. It does not acquire the shares of the business being sold.

nominated adviser (NOMAD)   The London Stock Exchange rules stipulate that each company wishing to join AIM must have a nominated adviser and broker. The nominated adviser is seen as having a key role in AIM companies, enjoying an ongoing advisory relationship as well as playing a monitoring role. The nominated adviser ensures that the AIM company is aware of its reporting and legal responsibilities.

ordinary shares   Ordinary shares give a shareholder no particular rights to share in the profits of a company. There is an entitlement to profits after other demands have been met, such as those of preference shareholders, but profits can be held in reserve by a company's directors. This is by far and away the most common type of share category in both quoted and unquoted companies.

overtrading   This is when a business runs out of cash, usually as a result of growing too fast. It happens because it runs out of working capital: customers don't pay on time, ever-increasing amounts of stock have to be bought (and paid for) to support growing sales, profit is reduced (or even non-existent) during this phase. The solution is to cut back growth to a level that can be financed and inject further working capital, eg bank loans, personal loans, additional equity.

preference shares   These give a shareholder a preferential right to share in the profits of a company before any payments are made to ordinary shareholders. Some preference shares are cumulative, so that profits missed in one year are paid in a subsequent year. These are the type of shares that venture capitalists or private equity houses will usually hold.

price earnings ratio (P/E ratio) or profit multiple   P/E ratios are used to value shares in both Stock Exchange quoted businesses and private businesses. The idea behind the P/E ratio is that it is a prediction or more likely an expectation of the company's performance in the future, dependent usually on market sector and company size. If a business has a P/E ratio of, say 10, and it has maintainable earnings of £500,000, then the business has a value of £5 million (10 x £500,000). 'Profit multiple' has the same meaning as P/E ratio but is used specifically for valuing unquoted businesses.

private equity house   Another name for a venture capitalist (*see* below).

prospectus, private placing   A private placing is generally a restricted offer to up to 50 individuals or institutions to purchase equity in a business or venture. As a private placing does not constitute a formal public offer of stock, the offer documents do not have to be in the form of a formal prospectus. A prospectus fulfils the same purpose as a private placing but is used where more than 50 individuals or institutions are being offered shares, eg a public flotation (IPO) or rights issue to existing shareholders.

redeemable preference shares   Redeemable preference shares may be a vehicle for dressing up debt as equity. As their name implies, the company has the right to redeem them, under terms specified on issue – usually at a future date. These shares give rights to a fixed dividend but generally have very limited voting rights and rank behind the ordinary creditors of the company but in priority to the ordinary shareholders. Used by venture capitalists and private equity houses as part of their quasi-debt funding, ie they get it back in a predetermined time.

rollover relief   A relief from capital gains tax (CGT), usually arising from the sale of a business, which means that either no CGT is payable or at worst it is delayed for several years. Rollover relief is available if the proceeds received from the sale of the asset are re-invested in new business assets, which do not have to be of the same category.

Small Firm Loan Guarantee Scheme (SFLGS)   SFLGS is a term loan arranged by all the main banks but guaranteed (up to 85 per cent) by the Department of Trade and Industry. It operates in exactly the same way as a term loan but with some important differences, one of which is that it cannot be used to replace existing loans (debt consolidation). It is specifically available to most SMEs that have a viable business proposition for which, because they do not have adequate security, they are unable to get bank funding. The security is provided by means of an insurance policy (which the borrower pays for).

small and medium-sized enterprise (SME)   A much used term describing those businesses that provide some 90 per cent of employment throughout Europe. The European Commission has defined this sector by the following criteria:

Category	Headcount	Turnover	Balance sheet total
Medium sized	<250	≤ €50 million	≤ €43 million
Small	< 50	≤ €10 million	≤ €10 million
Micro	< 10	≤ €2 million	≤ €2 million

Similar definitions are used by the Inland Revenue and Companies House.

trade sale   In many ways it is better and easier to sell to someone who already understands your type of business and industry. Who better than to sell to a supplier, customer or competitor – they already know the business, its track record, reputation, etc. Your business might fit in very well with their growth/diversification plans. This is what is known as a trade sale. Most businesses are sold by this route.

venture capitalist   Often rather unflatteringly referred to as 'venture capitalists'. A person, or more usually a business, that provides finance for businesses at any stage of its development. Usually the finance is in the form of equity, although they may offer mezzanine finance as well. They do not want to acquire or run the business they are investing in but want to share in the profit when it is sold on again. Venture capital firms usually have some limited involvement in the business, but this will vary from company to company. However, they will usually want a seat on the board, to influence strategic direction.

warranty   A warranty can be defined as a statement made in a contract, which if unfulfilled does not usually invalidate the contract but could lead to the payment of damages. If the warranty is clearly stated in writing it is known as an 'express warranty', and if it is not but is understood by both parties it is known as an 'implied warranty'.

working capital   Often referred to as the lifeblood of a business. This is the short-term money that is employed in a business's trading operations. It includes trading assets (also known as current assets) that the business needs to run its day-to-day business, eg stock, debtors and cash. Against these are those that have to be paid in the short term (known as current liabilities), eg suppliers, VAT and PAYE. The net of these (assets less liabilities) is referred to as 'working capital' or 'net current assets'.

Index

NB: page numbers in *italic* indicate figures or tables